by Brett Ortler

Adventure Publications
Cambridge, Minnesota

Dedication

To John, Jackie and Vicki Schaaf, and to Guy Sevenz, who is from Wisconsin.

Credits

Thanks to General Mills and Susan Wakefield, the Corporate Archivist for the General Mills Archives, for permission to use their images. Thanks also to Guy Gibbon, for his fine book, *Archaeology of Minnesota*.

Cover design by Lora Westberg and Jonathan Norberg

Book design by Jonathan Norberg

10 9 8 7 6 5 4
Minnesota Trivia Don'tcha Know!
Copyright © 2014 by Brett Ortler
Published by Adventure Publications, an imprint of AdventureKEEN
330 Garfield Street South, Cambridge, Minnesota 55008
(800) 678-7006
www.adventurepublications.net
All rights reserved. Printed in U.S.A
ISBN 978-1-59193-463-9 (pbk.)

Table of Contents

CANADA

Crookston

Moorhead

North
Dakota

South
Dakota

Pipestone

Alexandria

Minnesota River

Mississippi River

Minneapolis

St. Paul

Grand Rapids

Ely

Grand Marais

Duluth

Wisconsin

Rochester

Iowa

Introduction

From our (in)famous accent and Paul Bunyan to the notorious criminal past of St. Paul, Minnesota boasts an incredibly rich history and culture. Some of it is fascinating, some of it is funny, and some of it is just outright strange. This book is a representative look at the Land of 10,000 Lakes.

A mix of the silly and the serious, I've included everything from the standard fare of trivia books (the largest ball of twine! roadside sculptures!) to more serious but equally interesting tidbits about Minnesota. Learn some fascinating facts about our dreaded winter weather, famous crimes in state history, a history of disasters (natural and otherwise), and, of course, a look at our claims to fame: Minnesota's famous lakes and its portion of Lake Superior. And that's just a few of the topics!

Of course, it's impossible to know everything about Minnesota, let alone include it all in a single book. (To be sure, the histories of sports and music in Minnesota have entire trivia books dedicated to them!) In my view, that's a good problem: our state is simply too interesting!

And there are all sorts of tidbits to share. For example, did you know that St. Paul (page 90) was once the epicenter of the criminal underworld in the U.S.? Or that the port of Duluth-Superior (page 55) receives ocean-going ships, even though it's over 2,000 miles from the Atlantic Ocean? Or that plagues of locusts (page 81) descended upon much of Minnesota in the late 1800s?

You can find all of that and more in this book. It's my hope that this information will entertain you and inspire you to learn more about the wonderful state that Minnesotans call home.

A Glance at Minnesota (and Minnesotans)

The Great Seal of Minnesota

"Fairchild" the Gopher at the Minnesota State Fair

MINNESOTA IS HOME TO OVER FIVE MILLION PEOPLE, BUT A CLOSER LOOK AT THE STATE'S POPULATION PROVIDES A UNIQUE WINDOW ON THE STATE

NATIONAL STATUS: Minnesota existed as a territory from 1849 to 1858; it entered the Union as the 32nd state on May 11, 1858

POPULATION: 5,420,380[1]

HIGHEST POINT: Eagle Mountain, 2,301 feet above sea level

LOWEST POINT: Lake Superior, 601 feet above sea level

HIGHEST WATERFALL: The High Falls of the Pigeon River, 120 feet[2]

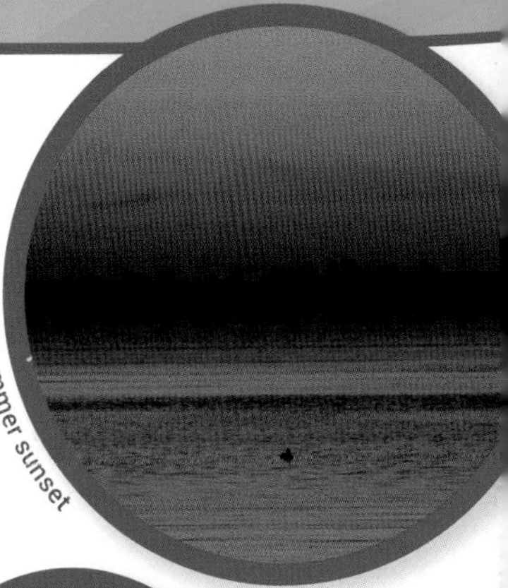

AREA, IN SQUARE MILES: 79,626.74, or about roughly the same area as the country of Belarus

NUMBER OF COUNTIES: 87

LARGEST CITY: Minneapolis, population 392,880[3]

CAPITAL: St. Paul, population 290,770

RACIAL DEMOGRAPHICS: White: 85.3 percent; Black or African American: 5.2 percent; American Indian or Alaska Native: 1.1 percent; Asian: 4.0 percent; Hispanic or Latino: 4.7 percent[4]

AGE BREAKDOWN: By 2020, there will be more people in Minnesota over the age of 65 than in the school-age population.[5]

BATTLE OF THE SEXES: According to the U.S. Census, females comprise 50.3 percent of Minnesota's population.[6] That means there are 162,611 more females than males, which is more than the population of Rochester, Minnesota's third-largest city.

CATS AND DOGS: Sadly, there is no official pet census.[7] (What a fun job that would be!) However, the American Veterinary Medical Service has compiled estimates of pets per capita. Using their estimates as a rough guide, there are probably about 760,000 Minnesotan households with at least one dog and 633,000 households owning a cat.

A summer sunset

The Minnesota State Capitol

TALLEST PERSON: Minnesota is home to one of the tallest people in the world. Igor Vovkovinskiy is a resident of Rochester and is 7 feet, 8.33 inches tall. Originally from Ukraine, he moved to Rochester to be treated for the pituitary disorder that caused his excessive height. Just how tall is he? Well, famed professional wrestler André the Giant was billed at 7' 4", but he was only really about 7 feet tall. (Later in life, he actually lost some height after a back surgery.[8]) So Mr. Vovkovinskiy has over eight inches on André the Giant—and he's over *two feet* taller than your humble author.

> **A FUN ANDRÉ THE GIANT STORY:** This is a bit of an aside, but it's too good not to tell. For a man billed at over 500 pounds, it's not surprising that André liked to eat; he especially liked to treat his friends to dinner. In one famous story, a friend tried to sneak away to pay the bill after dinner, only to find himself suddenly lofted into the air and placed back in his seat. That friend was none other than Arnold Schwarzenegger.[9]

OLDEST PERSON: One of the oldest Americans ever was from Minnesota. Walter Breuning was born in Melrose, Minnesota, on September 21, 1896, and he lived until April 14, 2011, reaching a staggering 114 years.[10] How old was he? He remembered the day President McKinley was shot, and he was later deemed too old to serve in World War II.

RICHEST PERSON: Several Minnesotans are among the Top 100 Richest Americans.[11] The wealthiest Minnesotans are Barbara Carlson Nelson and Marilyn Carlson Nelson. Heirs to the Carlson Group, each is worth approximately 3.9 billion dollars. According to the U.S. Census, median household income in Minnesota is about $58,000, meaning that their combined wealth could pay the median wage of approximately 134,000 people for one year.

MOST DENSELY POPULATED COUNTY: Ramsey, the state's smallest county, is also the most densely packed, with 3,280 people per square mile.[12] As you'd expect, Ramsey has nothing on Manhattan, which has a whopping 70,000 people per square mile.[13] But even Manhattan pales in comparison to Hong Kong's now-scrapped Kowloon Walled City, with its 3.25 *million* people per square mile.[14] If that's not enough, consider that the Kowloon Walled City was essentially built on the fly and its construction wasn't overseen by architects. Nonetheless, people went about their lives there for decades.

Kowloon Walled City

Paul Bunyan, Hot Dish and Other Minnesota Standards

Paul Bunyan statue

Tater tot hot dish

MINNESOTA IS KNOWN FOR PAUL BUNYAN, HOT DISH AND OUR NOTORIOUS ACCENT, BUT THERE IS MORE TO THESE FAMILIAR TOPICS THAN FIRST MEETS THE EYE

Paul Bunyan

Paul Bunyan was originally popularized by a lumber company

The details are murky, but the first Paul Bunyan stories reportedly circulated in logging camps and were passed along as loggers moved west. That's the traditional story, anyway. What really happened is more straightforward: A collection of Paul Bunyan stories was published in 1906 but failed to catch on until the Red River Lumber Company adopted Bunyan as their mascot. (The company was owned by none other than Thomas Walker, the founder of the Walker Art Museum.) The campaign was wildly popular, and the company even went so far as to publish a book of Paul Bunyan tales. Big Paul has been a staple of Minnesota lore ever since.

Paul Bunyan as depicted by the Red River Lumber Company

A Paul Bunyan grand tour in Minnesota

BEMIDJI: The Paul statue in Bemidji was originally packing heat, and real-life models were used for Paul and Babe

Bemidji's Paul Bunyan and Babe the Blue Ox statues have been a tourist destination since 1937. The Paul Bunyan statue was created using the mayor as the model, and the finished statue was scaled up by three to one. Paul's statue originally featured his shotgun, which lay next to him. It deteriorated, was removed and wasn't replaced.[1] When the Babe statue was created, a real ox was used as a model, then the statue was scaled up, just like with Paul.[2]

BRAINERD: Ever want to have a personal chat with Paul? You can

Once located in Brainerd proper, the city's famous Paul Bunyan statue is now located at Paul Bunyan Land outside Brainerd. The statue calls out each child's name as they approach (thanks to a handy microphone system), making it a family favorite. A large Babe the Blue Ox statue is also present, and the site features much more, including rides and many historic buildings.

BRAINERD: Was Paul Bunyan killed with a giant walleye?

According to one telling, he was. Brainerd is also home to a statue of Nanabozho, the Ojibwe trickster god and, in one story, Paul Bunyan's primary foe. Enraged when Bunyan clear-cut all the forests, Nanabozho fought him, eventually killing Paul by hitting him with a huge walleye.

AKELEY: Paul Bunyan's cradle and a Paul Bunyan statue that lends tourists a hand

Originally known as the home of the "Big Cradle" in which the infant Paul Bunyan originally slept, Akeley is now known for its 25-foot-tall statue of Paul. It features Bunyan kneeling down and holding out his hand as a make-shift chair, making for a great photo opportunity. (The cradle, which is still there, is likely a subtle nod to the fact that Akeley was the headquarters of the Red River Lumber Company, which helped popularize the Bunyan legend.)

The Paul Bunyan statue in Akeley

HACKENSACK: Did you know Paul Bunyan had a sweetheart?

Hackensack is home to Lucette, Paul Bunyan's sweetheart. Her full name is Lucette Diana Kensack, and she stands 17 feet tall. Built in 1991, her head fell off in a storm, but she was repaired (and given a somewhat different look) soon thereafter.

Paul Bunyan as an advertising pitchman

There are innumerable references to Paul Bunyan throughout the state. For example, Paul and Babe recently were the advertising pitchmen for MNSure, and if you look closely, the log flume ride at the Mall of America features a cameo of the pair. There is also a Paul Bunyan state trail and, somewhat ironically, a Paul Bunyan state forest.

The Lucette statue in Hackensack

The Minnesotan Accent

While many of us stridently deny it, Minnesotans do speak differently

Minnesotans share a distinct accent with our neighbors in Wisconsin, Iowa and the Dakotas. Not only do we use unique words—"hot dish" instead of "casserole"—we also pronounce our words differently. We say "car-mel" with two syllables instead of three; we say "creek" instead of "crik" and "Flore-ida" instead of "Flur-da" or other variants.[3] Many of our pronunciations stem from the long vowels in the languages of northern Europeans who settled in the region.

Did the movie *Fargo* cause a woman to die while searching for hidden gold?

Many of us blame the movie *Fargo* for highlighting the "Minnesotan" accent, but the movie is often said to have resulted in something much worse: the death of a Japanese woman who was allegedly seeking the film's buried cash.[4] This much is undisputed: In a postmodern flourish, the start of the film claims, "This movie is true." Five years after the movie was released, Takako Konishi traveled to Bismarck, then Fargo and died in a field outside Detroit Lakes. Because of a miscommunication with a police officer and her repetition of the word "Fargo," (she couldn't speak English and he couldn't speak Japanese) it was thought that she wanted to seek out the buried cash in the movie. As it turns out, the real story is less surreal, though no less dramatic: heartbroken after a bad breakup, she became depressed and decided to commit suicide in Minnesota, even sending a suicide note back home.

Hot Dish, Lutefisk and Other Foods

We really are a meat-and-potatoes people

In a survey, 130 Minnesotans were asked to prepare a representative dish from their area.[5] The resulting dishes usually featured meat (often beef) and potatoes in some form, and dessert was almost invariably a pie or some sort of bar. Traditional ethnic foods (of new immigrants and old alike) did make the list but were less common than one might think. Two Minnesota staples were well represented, however: wild rice and walleye.

The famous Fargo Theater

You knew hot dish was popular in Minnesota but what about in the halls of Congress?

Easily Minnesota's most famous dish, hot dish consists of a starch (often potatoes) mixed in with meat, vegetables (usually canned) and canned soup. All of this is then baked in one dish in an oven. Since 2010, Minnesota's congressional delegation has even held a yearly hot dish competition among its members.[6] Recent entries included Tim Walz's "Turkey Trot Tater Tot Hot Dish," which won, and Senator Amy Klobuchar's "It's So Cold My Hot Dish Froze," a dessert hot dish referencing our brutal winters.

Have a bundt cake pan? Thank a Minnesotan

Minnesotans didn't invent bundt cakes, which have their origins in Germany's Jewish population.[7] Nonetheless, a Minnesotan, H. David Dahlquist, did mass-produce the first bundt cake pan in the U.S. through his company, Nordic Ware. Since its release, over 60 million have sold.

More than seven billion cans of SPAM have been sold since 1937

Produced by Hormel Foods, SPAM consists of two types of pork meat mixed with sugar, salt, potato starch and sodium nitrate. Released in 1937, when the U.S. was still in the throes of the Great Depression, SPAM quickly became a go-to protein source, thanks to its long shelf life, portability and taste.[8] It was especially important as a food source for Allied Troops—over 100 million pounds were shipped to feed soldiers—and it soon caught on in Hawaii, Guam, the Philippines and other areas of the Pacific, where it is still quite popular. (Hawaii alone consumes 7 million cans each year.[9]) Since its creation, more than 7 billion cans of SPAM have been sold.

Let's talk about lutefisk: a truly terrifying food

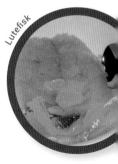

Lutefisk

A delicious fish, cod has long been a staple food in Scandinavia. Prior to the advent of refrigeration, cod that wasn't going to be eaten quickly had to be preserved. Drying was one way to preserve the fish. Unfortunately, lye is used in the drying process.[10] After the lye is applied, the fish is washed several times, and the resulting product is served with butter. In this writer's opinion, it turns a delicious vertebrate (a cod) into something like a long-deceased jellyfish. Still, many people in Minnesota enjoy it; Madison, Minnesota, is even known as the "Lutefisk Capital of the World" and boasts a statue of a cod that happens to be named Lou T. Fisk.

The Mill District at the turn of the century

Before we were the Mill City, we were Sawdust City

Minneapolis has rightfully been known as the Mill City thanks to its long ties to flour production, but before it was the Mill City, it was known as one of the primary sources of lumber in the country. The lumber, which originated in our then-pristine northern forests, was floated downstream on rivers, where it was processed at the many sawmills that soon sprang up. Unfortunately, the "limitless" forests were quickly clear-cut because there was no conception of resource management at the time. By the 1930s, the northern forests were essentially gone.

Mill City, then and now

Thanks to the waterpower provided by St. Anthony Falls, flour milling in Minneapolis boomed. By 1890, Minneapolis was producing more flour than any other city on the planet.[11] At its peak, Minneapolis produced 20,443,000 barrels in one year.[12] That was enough flour to make over six billion loaves of bread, or two for every person on earth at that time.[13] While many of the mills had closed down by the 1950s, General Mills is still going strong. Formed after the Washburn-Crosby Company (producers of the famous Gold Medal Flour) merged with a number of other mills, today, General Mills offers products that are famous worldwide and include everything from Cheerios to yogurts and Häagen-Dazs.

Milling references in Minnesota culture

A vintage Washburn-Crosby ad

If you look closely enough, you can see milling references all around the Twin Cities. Here are a couple you might not have known about:[14]

The Minneapolis Millers played professional baseball in Minnesota until 1960. Originally a professional team in a number of leagues, the Millers spent most of their career in the minor leagues, where they fielded a number of future Hall of Famers, including Willie Mays and Carl Yastrzemski.[15]

WCCO Radio's callsign stands for the Washburn-Crosby Company, which purchased the station in 1924. Renowned for its powerful signal, its broadcast can be picked up in Hawaii under the right conditions.[16]

From Malls to Mayo

Who invented shopping malls? We did

Minnesota is well known for its shopping malls. In fact, Southdale Center, which first opened in 1956 in Edina, was the first totally enclosed shopping center in the country. The mall remains open to this day and features some 120 stores.

A four-day spree, that's some serious power shopping

Anyone who knows anything about Minnesota has heard of the Mall of America. Many Minnesotans falsely claim it's the largest mall in the world, but believe it or not, it doesn't even crack the top 20. Sadly, it doesn't even rank as the largest mall in the U.S. (That title belongs to the King of Prussia Mall in Pennsylvania.) However, we Minnesotans can still be proud of our "mega-mall." Located in Bloomington, the Mall of America houses an amusement park, an aquarium, a movie theater and so much more—not to mention over 520 stores. In case that doesn't seem like a lot, consider this: if you were to spend just 10 minutes in each store, you'd shop for nearly four days straight without taking a single break!

Getting sick is no fun, but at least you're near a top hospital

Sure, the Mall of America attracts more visitors per year than Disney World. The state's other most famous attraction is far less fun but serves a much greater purpose. Rochester's Mayo Clinic is among the most acclaimed hospitals in the country. In fact, *U.S. News & World Report* ranks it the third-best hospital in the U.S., with top honors in such specialties as Diabetes & Endocrinology, Gynecology and Pulmonology.

We have the Mayo Clinic thanks to . . . the Civil War?

Dr. William Mayo came to the U.S. from England in 1846. He was assigned a position in 1864 in Rochester, Minnesota. His job? To examine recruits for the Union Army. Twenty-five years later, thanks in part to a tornado disaster, Dr. Mayo helped form what is now the Mayo Clinic.

Geology and Climate

Palisade Head

A glacier

WE TAKE MINNESOTA'S APPEARANCE FOR GRANTED, BUT THE STATE HAS CHANGED GREATLY: IT WAS HOME TO VOLCANOES AND GLACIERS AND WAS EVEN COVERED BY OCEANS!

Minnesota is (slowly) headed south. The state moves one inch to the south/southwest each year

When you look at a map of North America, it's easy to think of the continent as being static and unchanging. But that's not actually true. The continents that we see on the map are actually only part of larger structures called tectonic plates, which move very slowly over great lengths of time. Each year, the North American plate—including Minnesota—moves about one inch to the south/southwest. This means that if you fast-forward about 63,000 years, your house (and all of North America) will be about a full mile away from where it is now.

Minnesota once looked like California, then Indonesia

This constant motion means that Minnesota—and all land on Earth—is always a work in progress. According to the Minnesota Geological Survey, Precambrian Minnesota resembled modern-day Indonesia for a while; later, it resembled modern-day California, and still later, it resembled parts of the Middle East and eastern Africa.[1]

Lake Superior's rocky shores are the result of ancient lava flows

The various interactions of tectonic plates create the many geological phenomena we're familiar with, including everything from volcanoes and earthquakes to the formation of entire mountain ranges. Minnesota's geological history has been particularly active, and its effects are easy to see, even today. For example, Lake Superior's famous basalt shoreline was created when lava welled up after the North American continent tried (and failed) to break into two pieces about 1.1 billion years ago. This lava acted as a "patch" and prevented the rift from succeeding. If the rift had been successful, much of the land we

now call Minnesota would likely be at the bottom of a sea. Thankfully, the lava "patch" held; we directly benefit from this geological event in a number of other ways. Due to the weight of the new rock, a depression formed in the area. That depression would later become Lake Superior. Later, Lake Superior's famous agates formed in cavities in the cooled lava.

So much for the North Country: Minnesota was once in the Southern Hemisphere

We often think of Minnesota as the "North Country," and we take pride in our ability to endure (and enjoy) winter, but the climate we know and sometimes loathe is a relatively recent development. In fact, for much of its history, the land that we've come to call Minnesota was either underwater or in a different location altogether. In fact, if you go far enough back, parts of Minnesota weren't even in the Northern Hemisphere, as the equator cut through part of the state.[2]

Seashell hunting in the Twin Cities

A fossil brachiopod

What would become the Twin Cities was covered by a shallow freshwater sea in the Ordovician period, about 488 million years back. Some of the creatures that lived in that shallow sea fossilized and are easy to find today in the Twin Cities area. Would-be paleontologists can hunt for snail shells (gastropods), bivalves (brachiopods), fragments of sea lilies (crinoids) and the occasional trilobite. Trilobites were marine arthropods, distant relatives of today's crustaceans, insects and arachnids.

Minnesota's tragic absence of dinosaur fossils

Sadly, during the age of the dinosaurs, much of the land that would become Minnesota was essentially a swampy coastline.[3] Large reptiles swam in those seas, and dinosaurs roamed on the land that was present, but the rocks where they may have been buried are now located under thousands of feet of sediment or were "recycled" because of the Earth's constant geological processes.

Some of the oldest fossils on Earth are from Minnesota

If you want *old* fossils, head to Minnesota's Iron Ranges. Here you can find stromatolites, fossil remnants of blue-green algae.[4] Like the newer fossils you can find in the Twin Cities, these lived in an ocean, too, but that ocean was present about 1.5 billion years ago. Minnesota's stromatolites are some of the oldest fossils on Earth.

Lake Superior agates: hunting for Minnesota's state gemstone

Of course, Lake Superior agates are Minnesota's most famous geological specimens. Agates are a banded variety of chalcedony, a microcrystalline form of quartz.[5] Lake Superior's agates formed after vast swaths of lava cooled; gas seeping out of this lava left holes called vesicles in the rock. Later, water seeped in, depositing silica (quartz) and other minerals, especially iron, which produced the colorful red, orange and yellow bands that make agates so famous.

Moose Lake's record "Lake Superior agate" is actually chert

As durable as they are, most agates found today are relatively small and are generally no bigger than a walnut. Agates that reach a pound or greater are considered a once-in-a-life-time-find and are sometimes referred to as Lakers. Moose Lake's First National Bank claims to house the world's largest Lake Superior agate, a stone that weighs in at 108 pounds. Sadly, it's not actually an agate at all. It's banded chert.

Truckloads of gravel and agates, dumped onto a city street, lead to one fun scramble

Despite the too-good-to-be-true status of the fabled "largest" agate, Moose Lake rightfully bills itself as the "Agate Capital of the World" and hosts a weekend celebration called "Agate Days" every summer.[6] Agate Days features the famous "Agate Stampede," when over 300 pounds of agates and 300 dollars in quarters are mixed in with gravel and spread across one of the city's streets. A fun free-for-all ensues, with young and old alike digging in and looking for treasures.

Enjoying Agate Days in Moose Lake

Want to go agate hunting? You don't need to go to the North Shore. Agates can be found throughout much of the state

Since quartz is quite hard, agates are very durable; if they weren't, they wouldn't be nearly as common. After forming as much as a billion years ago, agates were subjected to millions of years of erosion followed by nature's bulldozers: the glaciers. The glaciers dislodged a wide variety of materials (including many agates) and transported them over a wide swath of the state. Areas near Lake Superior are best, but you don't have to be on the North Shore to find agates. Lake Superior gravel (and agates) can be found throughout much of the eastern half of Minnesota (and even in northern Iowa). Better yet, agate-bearing Lake Superior gravel is popular in landscaping and construction (even in the Twin Cities), so agates can be found in some seemingly unlikely places: in landscaping or roofing gravel, amid farm fields and on hiking trails in the middle of the forest. Most rock hounds search on the gravel beaches of Lake Superior, in gravel pits or on roadsides (especially in Carlton County). Some serious agate fans even scuba dive in Lake Superior to find the biggest agates. If you're looking on the beaches, it's best to look after a rough storm, as heavy waves replenish the agate crop.

A Lake Superior agate

Agates are one of Minnesota's gemstones, but they aren't the only ones

Because of their popularity and beauty, it's not surprising that agates are Minnesota's state gemstone. Nevertheless, agates aren't the only gemstone found in Minnesota; in fact, you can find several well-known gemstones and semi-rare metals in Minnesota, including amethyst (the traditional birth stone for February), copper and one of Minnesota's most elusive minerals, thomsonite.

Thunder Bay amethyst

TRIVIA TIDBIT: There are several cups that are alleged to be the Holy Chalice (the cup that Christ used at the Last Supper). One of the cups—and arguably the one with the most likely provenance—resides in the Cathedral of Valencia in Spain.[7] So why am I mentioning it here? It's made of agate.

Thomsonite: another Lake Superior treasure

Thomsonite is a type of zeolite (a group of silica/quartz minerals), and it is as rare as it is famous.[8] Thomsonite was named for the Scottish chemist Thomas Thomson, who identified it in the nineteenth century. Like agates, most thomsonite specimens are quite small, but they are sought after for their characteristic coloration, especially pale pinks, reds and greens. Thomsonite specimens often feature "eyes," circular rings that make thomsonite popular for use in jewelry, especially rings, earrings and necklaces.

Where to go to hunt for thomsonite

In Minnesota, you might find scattered pieces up and down the North Shore, but two beaches are particularly well-known for thomsonite. If you're interested, book a night at Thomsonite Beach (a private resort) or visit Cutface Creek (a public wayside just south of Grand Marais, Minnesota).

Queen Victoria: a famous fan of thomsonite?

Queen Victoria

Thomsonite had some fairly famous fans; when the original thomsonite deposits in Scotland were depleted, Queen Victoria reportedly hired Ojibwe Indians near Grand Marais to find thomsonite for her.[9] To this day, it's popular in jewelry, and fine specimens are quite valuable.

TRIVIA TIDBIT: Pipestone, Minnesota, is known for its famous "pipestone," which is found at Pipestone National Monument. The soft, red stone (also known as Catlinite) is ideal for carving, and has been used for centuries by American Indian cultures in peace pipes and other carvings. Pipestone collecting is restricted to those of American Indian descent.

Want to see some of Minnesota's other impressive geological sights? Head underground!

When many people think of caves, they think of New Mexico's famous Carlsbad Caverns and Lechuguilla Cave, but Minnesota has a number of impressive caves, including Mystery Cave, a 13-mile-long cave located near the Iowa border. Administered by the state park system, regular walking tours are offered, as are down-and-dirty "real caving" trips. Southeastern Minnesota is also home to Niagara Cave, which features fossils embedded in its walls, a spectacular water-gouged "hallway" and even a wedding chapel.[10] Closer to the metro area, you can visit the Wabasha Street Caves, which are actually mines gouged out of the St. Peter Sandstone; over the course of the last 150 years, they've been used to grow mushrooms and have housed speakeasies and the Castle Royale, a once-resplendent 1930s-era restaurant. Today, they are home to an underground dance hall that features swing music and tours dedicated to mobsters, ghosts and the criminal history of the Twin Cities.[11]

Niagara Cave

Minnesota gold rushes

When it comes to mining, Minnesota may be known primarily for its iron ore, but in its early days, Minnesota was the site of two gold rushes. Both focused on the North Country. One occurred near Lake Vermillion in 1865, producing almost no gold but spurring the development of iron mining in the region.[12] The second gold rush took place in 1893 near Rainy Lake. Several mines actually produced some gold, though they soon went bankrupt. That may not be the end of the story for gold mining in Minnesota, however. A number of companies are surveying for precious metals in Minnesota, and one proposed mine, if approved, would extract nickel and cobalt, as well as palladium, gold and silver from northern Minnesota.[13]

A gold nugget

Petroglyphs: a window into Minnesota's American Indian history

Not all of Minnesota's interesting geological features were produced by Mother Nature. Minnesota has been home to a number of American Indian tribes for millennia prior to European settlement. Most of us are familiar with the Dakota (also known by the disparaging term Sioux) and the Ojibwe (also known as the Chippewa), and both groups still reside in the state today. Petroglyphs are one of the most enduring—and fascinating—mysteries left behind by Minnesota's early American Indian populations. Consisting of symbols or drawings carved into stone, these ancient markings can be found throughout the state, from Jeffers in the southwest to the Boundary Waters Canoe Area Wilderness.

Climate

One state but four different habitats

As anyone who has taken a road trip across the state can tell you, the scenery changes quite a bit depending on where you are. (In this respect, we are the anti-Nebraska.) Each of these "scenery changes" corresponds with a biological biome, and there are four types in Minnesota.[14] The extreme northwest of the state consists of grassy parklands and scattered aspen stands. Most of the North Country is rocky and replete with pine trees and lakes; if you head farther south, the forests eventually become dominated by oak. Head farther still, and you'll enter the prairie country. Most of the former prairie is now agricultural land; only one percent of the original prairie remains.[15]

> **TRIVIA TIDBIT:** Settlers originally thought the prairie land was lousy farmland. Part of the problem was that the wooden or cast-iron plows of the time were no match for the tough soil. After metal plows became reliable, settlers quickly realized that the prairie land was some of the most productive farmland on the planet. The inventor of that new-fangled plow was none other than John Deere himself.[16]

Tallgrass prairie

Minnesota's biomes change over time

If you traveled back in time 5,000 years, you probably wouldn't recognize Minnesota as Minnesota.[17] This isn't because of the vagaries of erosion or sediment deposition; the differences were much more profound—the ecosystem was different and the boundaries between biomes were different than they are now. Consider Isanti County as an example. Located about an hour north of the Twin Cities, Isanti County is covered by deciduous forest today. About 13,000 years ago, it was covered by spruce forest, and 9,000 years ago, it was covered by prairie.[18] Those aren't small changes; on the contrary, each of those biomes is home to different groups of plants and animals.

You think it's cold now...you should have seen 13,000 years ago

The landscape isn't the only thing that has changed. Over time, Minnesota's climate has varied significantly. For example, according to climate models, Minnesota would have been much colder 13,000 years ago, just after the most recent ice age ended.[19] Baudette's mean temperature in January was predicted to have been -16 degrees.[20] That's sixteen degrees colder than the average temperature in January today. Such an environment has more in common with the arctic than it does with Minnesota.[21] That's the climactic equivalent of a latitude shift of 20 degrees or a thousand miles north. Thankfully, things warmed up later on, making the area (at least somewhat) inhabitable in the winter.

Minnesota's warming climate

Thanks to a century of carbon dioxide emissions, Minnesota, like the rest of the world, is warming. We're already seeing impacts of climate change.[22] For example, the USDA recently revised its famous hardiness zone map, which is based on an area's lowest average winter temperature. Those temperatures are slowly rising, so some plants can now survive where they likely would have perished before; many areas in Minnesota are now a full zone warmer than listed on the 1990 map.[23]

Weather, Winter and Natural Disasters

A tornado outside LeSeur

MINNESOTA HAS SEEN EVERYTHING FROM TORNADOES TO WINTER STORMS WITH HURRICANE-FORCE WINDS. ON A NUMBER OF OCCASIONS, OUR WILD WEATHER HAS TAKEN A HEAVY HUMAN TOLL

Tower versus Embarrass: a competition to claim the title of coldest city in Minnesota

Minnesotans revel in the winter—so much so that two Minnesotan cities, Tower and Embarrass (yes, that's a real name), hold a contest each year to see which records the coldest winter temperature. The current leader is Tower, which holds the state record of -60 F, set on February 2, 1996. OK, that's cold, but we have hats with ear flaps, so we can handle it. However, -60 F is downright balmy when you compare it to the coldest temperature recorded on Earth, which was just about -128 F. Guess where? Yes, Antarctica. (Vostok Station, to be exact.) That's a 68-degree difference and 160 degrees below freezing.

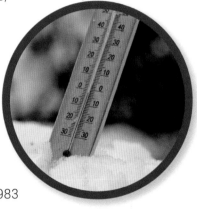

Weather extremes in Minnesota[1]

Hottest recorded temperature: 115 degrees F, Beardsley, 1917

Coldest recorded temperature: -60 degrees F, Tower, 1996

Most rainfall in 24 hours: 15.1 inches, Hokah, 2007

Most snow in 24 hours: 36 inches, Finland, 1994

Most snow from one storm: 46.5 inches, Finland, 1994

Maximum recorded wind speed: 117 miles per hour, Alexandria, 1983

This is why you always bring a coat: sometimes the temperature can drop 71 degrees in less than a day

As Minnesotans, we know our weather can be fickle. Temperature swings of 30 degrees in a day are common, and if conditions are right, an unseasonably warm day can quickly turn into an unseasonably cold day.[2] On rare occasions, the swings can be incredibly pronounced. The worst 24-hour swing happened in Lamberton, Minnesota, when the temperature went from an outright warm 78 degrees to 7 degrees after a cold front swept in on April 3, 1982. One wonders how many umbrella-drinks were hastily abandoned on suddenly freezing porches.

The snowiest winters in the Twin Cities[3]

98.6 inches: 1983-84
95.0 inches: 1981-82
88.9 inches: 1950-51
86.6 inches: 2010-11
84.9 inches: 1916-17
84.1 inches: 1991-92
81.3 inches: 1961-62
79.0 inches: 1951-52
78.4 inches: 1966-67
75.8 inches: 2000-01

In Minnesota, there's usually a good chance of a white Christmas, but some places are better than others

It shouldn't be surprising that snowy Christmases are common in Minnesota, but Minnesota doesn't always have a white Christmas. In fact, there is no snow on the ground at Christmas in the Twin Cities about once every four years.[4] Of course, some areas of the state are far snowier than others, so snow cover at Christmas varies significantly by region. In the North Country (near Cook, for example), a white Christmas is almost certain, but in St. Peter, a white Christmas happens only 59 percent of the time.[5]

The coldest* winters in the Twin Cities (daily average)[6]

3.7°: 1874-1875

5.8°: 1886-1887

7.1°: 1935-1936

8.1°: 1872-1873

8.4°: 1903-1904

8.4°: 1916-1917

9.2°: 1882-1883

9.4°: 1978-1979

9.7°: 2013-2014

*For comparison, 18 F is average.

International Falls fought a legal battle to retain the title of "Icebox of the Nation"

Of course, given how much Minnesota's climate and geography vary, snowfall and temperature records often differ significantly in other parts of the state. Nonetheless, some cities are consistently cold. International Falls is certainly one of them. The inspiration for Frostbite Falls, the home of the cartoon characters Rocky and Bullwinkle, International Falls does have downright cold weather, but its nickname is a bit of an exaggeration, as there are many places in northern Minnesota with colder record temperatures.

Oddly, International Falls had to fight in court for the right to call itself the nation's icebox, as the city of Fraser, Colorado, claimed that it held the legal right to the trademark. International Falls eventually prevailed in 2008 and now can exclusively use the nickname.[7]

The official "Icebox of the Nation"

In an average year in Minnesota, we get snow in fall, winter and spring

If you ever felt like winter was never-ending, you weren't all that wrong. In the Twin Cities, the average date of the first inch of snowfall is November 22; the average date of the last snowfall is April 2.[8] This means that Minnesota's "winter" extends into fall and spring, and that's just in an average year. If we're really unlucky, snow can even fall in August or September.

Ever feel like it's always below zero in January? Sometimes, that's almost true

In 1912, the average temperature for the month of January was -2.7 F.[9] This doesn't mean it was below zero the entire time, but if you look at the 1912 records, you wouldn't want to have gone through it. For the first 12 days of the month, only one day was above zero, and the temperature stayed below zero for a full *seven* days.[10] And the days surrounding that were no picnic. The cold snap was only broken because of a slight "warm snap." The temperature? A balmy 2 degrees.

The worst winter of all time? For cold, it was 1874-1875

When it comes to sheer cold, the winter of 1874-1875 has it beat.[11] The entire month was below freezing, and a whopping 21 days saw lows of -10 F or below, and 10 days were -20 or colder. The coldest lows occurred on the 8th and the 9th, when the temps reached -30 below. And the highs weren't much to look forward to. In January and February, the average daily temperatures were -3.4 F and -2.6 F, respectively. Ouch. This makes the recent winter of 2014 positively tame by comparison; in the Twin Cities in 2014, the January/February averages were 8.0 and 8.6, respectively.[12]

TRIVIA TIDBIT: International Falls has never hit 100 degrees in the summer.[13]

Good news: It doesn't snow here in July! The bad news? It still might be freezing

Snow has never been recorded in Minnesota in July, but it has been recorded in every other month.[14] Still, don't break out your flip-flops and Hawaiian shirts just yet; even a cursory look at the minimum temperature records makes it clear that cities across Minnesota can occasionally be darn cold (at or below freezing), even in summer. Tower holds the record lows for July and August, with lows of 24 and 21, respectively.

On fishing opener, sometimes the lake is covered in ice!

For many Minnesotans, fishing opener is an important date on the calendar, as it marks the beginning of cabin season and the start of summer. Unfortunately, the weather doesn't always cooperate. Fishing amid snow flurries isn't unheard of, and sometimes in the North Country, the lakes are still covered in ice. In 1966, Gunflint Lake in Cook County didn't shed its ice until May 26.[15] In the southern half of the state, most lakes usually lose their ice in late March and early April. Northern lakes usually lose their ice in the last two weeks of April. Only the northernmost lakes continue to be ice-covered beyond the first week of May.[16]

It once rained frogs in Northeast Minneapolis

Sometimes, it doesn't just rain water. On July 4, 1901, *The Minneapolis Tribune* reported, "It rained frogs in Northeast Minneapolis the other day, and the residents of that neighborhood sat up half the night waiting for the fishing tackle to come down."[17] A strong thunderstorm was actually to blame.

Blizzards

The Children's Blizzard of 1888 killed hundreds, including many children

Perhaps the most infamous blizzard in the history of the Midwest, the Schoolchildren's Blizzard gets its name for the large number of schoolchildren it killed.[1] The blizzard, just one

of many that struck the region that year, hit suddenly on January 12. Almost immediately, the temperature plummeted nearly 20 degrees and kept dropping. Blowing snow soon piled up, creating huge drifts and reducing visibility to next to nothing. Temperatures reached 30 below zero and even 40 below, farther west. The storm hit the hardest in the Dakotas and in Nebraska, though western Minnesota was not unscathed. Because of how suddenly it came on, many people were stuck out in the storm, and the combination of the incredible cold and zero visibility led many victims to lose their way and literally freeze solid, sometimes just feet from their homes. Many of the victims were schoolteachers or students who got lost while attempting to make their way home. Because records were scattered, the complete death toll is unknown, but somewhere between 250 and 500 people[2] died throughout the region.

The Armistice Day Blizzard of 1940 killed dozens of unsuspecting hunters

Another storm that struck without warning, the Armistice Day Blizzard hit during the height of duck hunting season. Because of the unseasonably warm temperatures—38 degrees[3]—hunters went out wearing relatively light clothing. At first, they had good luck, as vast flocks of ducks were in the air. Soon, however, the wind came up, temperatures plummeted, and snow reduced visibility to next to nothing. By the end of the storm, the region had seen hurricane-force gusts, and more than 16 inches of snow had fallen in Minneapolis. Other parts of the state reported much more snow, up to 26 inches.[4] By the end of the blizzard, 49 Minnesotans died, and many others perished in neighboring states.[5]

Minnesota's Storm of the Century shut down the entire state for over a week

When a storm hits Minnesota, it's not rare for affected highways to become impassable for a day or two, but closures to interstates are relatively rare. The blizzard that hit Minnesota from January 10 to 12 in 1975 was so bad it closed most of the roads in the entire *state*.[6] Snow totals varied wildly across Minnesota, but the whole of the state was blasted by high winds (with gusts in excess of 80 mph). This created drifts up to 20 feet high in Duluth;

farther south, the roads were impassable because of the wind and ice.[7] The high winds led to dangerous wind chills, and by the time it was over, 58 deaths were attributed to the storm. Many heart attack deaths were also reported as people dug out of the snow.[8]

This winter may really be the end of you: shoveling snow might lead to heart attacks

When winter gets particularly bad, Minnesotans often joke that the lousy weather will be the end of us. In some cases, that might actually be true.[9] Cardiologists have studied the alleged correlation between shoveling snow and heart attacks, and there is some evidence that the sudden exertion necessary to move mountains of snow might be enough to trigger a heart attack in members of the population with certain characteristics (sedentary lifestyle, undiagnosed heart disease). While it's not clear if a connection exists, the idea definitely doesn't seem far-fetched.

The Halloween Blizzard of 1991 hit Minnesota thanks to the Perfect Storm on the East Coast

While 1991 was a good year for the Minnesota Twins, it was a bad year for storms. The East Coast was hit by the infamous Perfect Storm (a combination of a nor'easter' and a Category 2 Hurricane). The Midwest, including much of Minnesota, was thwacked by the Halloween Blizzard. Oddly, without the Perfect Storm, it's unlikely that the Halloween Blizzard would have struck Minnesota. The storm originally developed in Texas but couldn't travel east because it was blocked by the atmospheric front of the Perfect Storm.[10, 11] The storm was therefore forced to head north. Starting just as trick-or-treaters were making their way around Minnesota neighborhoods, the storm quickly picked up in intensity. Over the course of four days, it dropped two to three feet of snow on parts of Minnesota. Minneapolis-St. Paul saw a record 28.4 inches of snow, and Duluth saw 36.9 inches. The storm also knocked out power in rural areas and created glare ice on roads across the state, leading to the deaths of 20 people.[12]

Droughts and Dust Storms

The Dust Bowl strikes Minnesota during the "Decade from Hell"

While the Dust Bowl is often associated with Oklahoma and Texas, it affected the country as a whole, and Minnesota was no exception.[1] (Dust storms reached Minneapolis in 1934 and even reached as far east as Washington, D.C.[2]) The years from 1929 to 1939 were rife with drought, crop failures and extreme summertime temperatures that were perversely followed up by a number of brutal winters. Crops were buried in dust, and dying plants simply withered away in the heat. When rain did come, it often came in one fell swoop amid severe weather, often doing as much harm as good. This decade of meteorological aberrations unfortunately coincided with the Great Depression, making an already desperate situation much worse. In short, everything that could go wrong seemingly did, both in Minnesota and elsewhere.[3] In areas subjected to dust storms, this led to many reported cases of "dust pneumonia," which led to a number of deaths. (The disease even figured into a Woody Guthrie folk song.[4])

While the exact impact of the Decade from Hell is impossible to compute, the heat waves, crop failures and resulting malnutrition took a great human toll and added to the misery of the Great Depression in Minnesota.[5]

Dust storms like this one (in South Dakota) affected Minnesota

The Drought of 1988

Another famous drought hit Minnesota 50 years later. While the human costs of the drought were far less pronounced than in the Great Depression, meteorologically speaking, it was a doozy. June saw an average of just 1.4 inches of rainfall statewide, the lowest ever, and things didn't get better in July.[6] Crop yields crashed, sprinkling bans were enforced across the state, and perhaps most noticeably, it was blisteringly hot outside. The temperature was consistently well above average; half of the days in the month reached 85 degrees or higher.[7]

Tornadoes

Not far from Tornado Alley

Situated just north of Tornado Alley, Minnesota averages 27 tornadoes a year, though some years have many more. Twisters are most common in May, June and July.[1] (No tornadoes have ever been reported between December and February.) Prior to the rise of modern weather forecasting and electronic communication, deaths by tornado were relatively common. Today, they are quite rare; the last time more than one person died from a tornado was in 1993.[2]

The deadliest tornado in Minnesota's history hit Sauk Centre, killing 72

The deadliest tornado to strike Minnesota hit St. Cloud and Sauk Centre on April 14, 1886. Retroactively rated as an F4 tornado, the second-strongest classification, the tornado absolutely leveled the city of Sauk Centre, destroying the courthouse and every business in town, and it tossed a fully loaded freight train into the air, turning its cars into "shapeless masses."[3] The twister, which was described as being incredibly dark in coloration, left a path of destruction 330 feet wide for 20 miles. In the process, it snatched people into the air, and the bodies were described as having a blackened, almost scorched appearance; many had their clothes torn from their bodies by the winds. In the end, 72 people died. Sauk Centre, a town that seemingly had a bright future, experienced a setback that took decades to recover from.[4]

The headline in St. Paul after the tornado struck

VOL. VIII.

CALAMITY

The Wicked Demon of the Clouds Descends

Upon the Cities of St. Cloud and Sauk Rapids,

...thlessly Crushes

The worst tornadoes to hit the Twin Cities: the 1965 Fridley/Minneapolis twisters

There are many myths about tornadoes, but one of the most common is that tornadoes can't hit urban areas. As the tornadoes that hit Salt Lake City, Miami and even New York City have shown, tornadoes can—and do—strike metro areas. The Twin Cities have been hit on a number of occasions. The worst outbreak occurred on May 6, 1965, when a series of five tornadoes—three reaching F4 in intensity—tore through the Twin Cities area, killing 13 and injuring 683.[5]

Anoka and Carver Counties were especially hard hit; thankfully, meteorologists and radio and television news stations were able to provide some advance warning. The outbreak saw an important first: the storm marked the first time the civil defense air raid sirens were used to warn residents of an impending tornado.[6]

The 2011 North Minneapolis tornado

Another major storm struck on May 22, 2011, when an F-1 or F-2 tornado hit North Minneapolis.[7] The storm damaged nearly 4,000 buildings and killed two people.[8] Unfortunately, damage from the tornado has lingered for several years.[9]

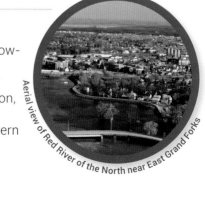

The aftermath of the North Minneapolis twister

Anoka and St. Peter: two cities synonymous with tornadoes

Some cities in Minnesota are famous for their run-ins with tornadoes, and Anoka and St. Peter are certainly two of them. The largest tornado to hit Anoka struck in 1939, killing 9 and injuring over 200.[10] Anoka has since embraced the image; its high school mascot is now the tornado. St. Peter, on the other hand, was hit by an F-3 tornado, which destroyed portions of Gustavus Adolphus College.

Floods and Other Storms

The 1997 Red River Flood: a once-in-a-century flood

The Red River is something of an oddity—it flows north.[1] Flowing from its headwaters on the border of North Dakota and Minnesota (near Breckenridge), its waters eventually empty into Hudson Bay. Unfortunately for the residents of the region, this geographical quirk exacerbates flooding on the river, especially when there is heavy snowfall, because the southern

Aerial view of Red River of the North near East Grand Forks

portions of the river thaw first and the water backs up, only to later inundate the northern portions of the river. That's what happened in 1997. The previous autumn had been abnormally wet, and the winter was replete with blizzards. When the thaw finally came, the region began to flood. In all, several cities were hit—floodwaters in Fargo-Moorhead were over 20 feet above flood stage, and Grand Forks saw water 26 feet over flood stage.[2] This was significantly higher than the National Weather Service forecast, and the levies that had been built soon breached, inundating much of Grand Forks and East Grand Forks. While no one was killed, it proved to be one of the most expensive disasters in the region's history, costing over five billion dollars.

The Sorlie Bridge flooding near East Grand Forks

1987 Superstorm: the heaviest rainfall in Twin Cities history

The storm, which occurred from July 23 to July 24, 1987, dumped an astounding 10 inches of rain in 8 hours on the Twin Cities.[3] As you might expect, this led to serious flooding, with some stretches of roadways turning into rivers. I-494 flooded to a depth of up to eight feet, and two people were killed.[4] The storm caused a whopping $30 million dollars in damage (about $60 million today).[5]

The derecho of 1999 leveled 25 million trees in the BWCAW

Most severe storms are ephemeral, but a derecho is different. A boomerang-shaped line of thunderstorms with consistently strong winds, a derecho is persistent and can travel hundreds of miles, subjecting everything in its path to a barrage of heavy winds. On July 4, 1999, a derecho traveled from North Dakota through Minnesota's Boundary Waters Canoe Area Wilderness and into Canada. Wind speeds were estimated to have reached 100 mph in Minnesota, terrifying many campers and leveling tens of millions of trees in what is often referred to as the "1999 Blowdown."[6] Evidence of the storm is still visible today in the BWCAW, though re-growth has begun to bury the remnants of the storm damage.

Earthquakes

The strongest earthquake in recorded history in Minnesota: a 5.0, nothing to sneeze at but nothing Californians aren't familiar with

When we think of natural disasters in Minnesota, we usually think of tornadoes or blizzards or strong windstorms. Earthquakes don't usually make the list, but even though Minnesota is far removed from any major fault lines, earthquakes still do occur every so often. Clocking in at 5.0 on the Richter Scale, the strongest recorded earthquake occurred near Morris, Minnesota, in 1975, producing minor damage to houses and structures.[1]

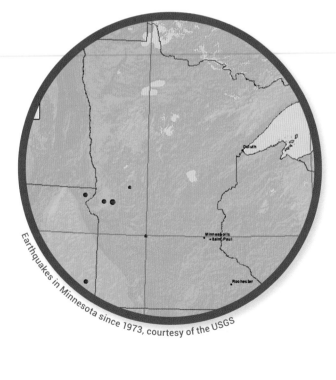

Earthquakes in Minnesota since 1973, courtesy of the USGS

Wildlife

A bull moose

Common Loon

WITH THOUSANDS OF BEARS AND WOLVES, MINNESOTA IS A WILDLIFE HAVEN, SO GET TO KNOW OUR WILD NEIGHBORS (AND I DON'T MEAN PEOPLE FROM WISCONSIN)

The common loon: a bird that needs a runway

Minnesota's state bird, the Common Loon is actually only a resident in Minnesota part of the time. Loons spend their winters in the southern coastal regions; Minnesota's loons often head to the Gulf of Mexico.[1] Nonetheless, when they are here, they make their presence known, as their haunting calls echo throughout the summer nights. Incredibly clumsy on land, loons need a runway of water to take off. (They can't take off from land.) In this respect, loons are essentially nature's float planes, but once they get in the air, they can fly quite quickly—topping out at about 70 miles per hour.[2]

Once a rarity, eagle populations are booming in Minnesota

Once heralded as something of a miraculous product, the pesticide DDT led to serious declines in the nation's bald eagle population (among other species).[3] American Bald Eagles were already threatened due to hunting, which was legal at the time, and by the mid 1960s, there were only a few dozen nesting populations left in the entire country. Restrictions on the use of DDT helped bald eagles recover, and today Minnesota alone is home to over 1,300 pairs of eagles.[4]

Up north, bears make bird feeding a lot more interesting

There may be as many as 30,000 black bears in Minnesota, and it's not entirely uncommon to spot a bear at a state park or one ambling across a backcountry road.[5] Sometimes, the encounters are a lot more personal than that; this is especially true if you leave out bird feeders. Bears are not picky eaters, and it's not rare to find a bear cub hanging happily from a suet feeder or to see a momma bear to knock down a feeder. While black bears are at the top of the food chain today, they were once hunted by much larger animals (including bigger bears!). Thankfully for us, this made them skittish, and they can usually be scared off by something as intimidating as a feisty dachshund. While attacks are not unheard of, your bird feeder is a far more likely target. Folks up north are advised to bring in their feeders at night and to put them

where only birds can reach them. (Intentionally feeding bears can make them more likely to approach humans and therefore potentially more dangerous.)

The number of serious wolf attacks in recorded Minnesota history? One

Aside from Alaska, Minnesota has the most gray wolves in the U.S. While wolf attacks in Europe aren't unheard of, attacks in North America are incredibly rare. In fact, the first recorded wolf attack in Minnesota occurred in 2013, when a teenager out camping with his girlfriend was attacked by a wolf, which essentially latched onto his head.[6] He managed to fight off the wolf and was treated for his wounds at a nearby hospital. The wolf, which was later killed, was found to have serious abnormalities—including dental issues and brain damage—that likely led it to have trouble feeding.[7]

Want to know the most dangerous animal in the state? The white-tailed deer

Bear attacks are incredibly rare, and wolf attacks almost never occur. So what is the most dangerous animal in Minnesota? It might surprise you: the white-tailed deer. There are an estimated one million white-tailed deer throughout Minnesota—nearly twice the population of both Minneapolis and St. Paul. (If they were all centered in one place there would be a veritable deer metropolis.) Those deer are often on the move—leading to about 20,000 crashes each year.[8] Some of these crashes cause serious injuries, and deer-vehicle crashes (often involving motorcycles) even lead to a handful of deaths in Minnesota each year.[9, 10]

Sadly, moose populations are crashing

In Minnesota, moose are found in two areas: along the North Shore and in the northwestern portion of the state. The state's moose population is a major tourist draw, and "watch for moose" signs are common as one heads north along Highway 61. Unfortunately, Minnesota's moose population has dropped by over 50 percent since 2010, and it appears to be in significant trouble.[11] While data is still being collected, one credible hypothesis is that Minnesota's warming climate is having an impact on moose, which are quite sensitive to warm weather. If that's true, then moose populations may be the first Minnesotan victims of climate change.[12]

Orchids, carnivorous plants and cacti: plants you might not expect in Minnesota

Minnesota's plant community is incredibly diverse and includes some surprising and exotic finds. Minnesota is rich with orchids; 43 orchid species are found in the state.[13] The most famous is undoubtedly the Showy Lady's Slipper, the state flower. While the state's orchids are rightfully famous, Minnesota also boasts a number of carnivorous species, 13 in all. The most widespread is the pitcher plant. As you'd expect, it resembles a narrow pitcher of water; insects are lured into the pitcher by nectar glands in the plant.[14] Once inside, the insect is trapped and eventually drowns in the pool of water at the bottom of the pitcher. It's then digested by the plant, which derives nutrients from the insect. The pitcher plant is arguably not the most surprising plant in Minnesota: a species of prickly pear cactus can be found in the southwest reaches of the state.[15]

TRIVIA TIDBIT: Minnesota is even home to a bioluminescent (glow-in-the-dark) mushroom species. Appropriately enough, it is named the jack-o-lantern mushroom.[16]

The Showy Lady's Slipper, Minnesota's State Flower

Minnesota's 10,000 Lakes

MINNESOTA IS FAMOUS FOR ITS LAKES, AND RIGHTFULLY SO. OUR LAKES ARE ENJOYED BY CANOEISTS IN THE BOUNDARY WATERS, KIDS FISHING OFF THE DOCK AND EVERYONE IN BETWEEN

Minnesota is actually the Land of 11,842 Lakes

Our license plates don't exaggerate; if anything, they are a bit modest. There are actually more than 10,000 lakes in Minnesota. According to the DNR, there are 11,842 lakes of at least 10 acres.[1] Of the 87 counties in Minnesota, four didn't chip in a single natural lake at all. The four counties are Mower, Olmsted, Pipestone and Rock counties.

Manitoba has ten times as many lakes as Minnesota

Believe it or not, Manitoba is known as "the land of 100,000 lakes," which is no exaggeration.[2] Then again, huge swaths of northern Manitoba lack access to roads, so while Manitoba may have more lakes, most of ours are much easier to access.

When you add in Minnesota's wetlands, rivers and streams, over one fourth of Minnesota is covered in water

A wetland near Isanti, Minnesota

The combined area of all Minnesota's lakes, rivers, wetlands and streams covers 13 million acres of land in Minnesota. Minnesota is often alleged to have more shoreline than California, Florida and Hawaii combined, but as it turns out, that's not entirely true.[3] According to one analysis, our 44,000 miles of shoreline do beat the combo of California and Hawaii, but when you add in Florida, the trio wins.

TRIVIA TIDBIT: At 2,320 miles, the Mighty Mississippi River is the fourth-longest river in the world. As any good Minnesotan knows, it gets its start at Itasca State Park.

Prior to European settlement, Minnesota had about twice as many wetlands

Minnesota currently has about 10.6 million acres of wetlands, but it used to have far more, about 20 million acres.[4] Farmers and city planners quickly set about draining these wetlands and converting them for other uses. Just how much have we changed the state? Well, consider that Minnesota has over 21,200 miles of ditches.[5] That's right, ditches. To put that in perspective, Minnesota has 92,000 miles of natural rivers and streams.[6]

TRIVIA TIDBIT: All of Minnesota's earthworms went extinct during the last glacial period, so every wiggler you see today is a relative of one that was introduced, usually in soil for gardens or even as released fishing bait. That might not sound important, but earthworms have changed the landscape tremendously: they consume the leaf litter that gathers on the forest floor. This leaf litter acts as a natural fertilizer; without it, many native species—including pine seedlings—have a much more difficult time growing.

With more than 10,000 lakes, some of the names get repetitive; others are outright odd

With so many lakes in Minnesota, it's not surprising that many of them have the same name. The most common[7] names are rather uninspired: Mud, Long, Rice, Bass, Round and so on. Then again, some lakes have pretty odd names. Itasca State Park is home to a Coffee Break Lake, and the Boundary Waters Canoe Area Wilderness is home to some strange names, including Misplaced Lake, Tin Can Mike Lake and the rather unfortunately named Wench Lake, Little Johnson Lake and Bogus Lake.[8] My favorite BWCAW lake name isn't a lake at all: it's Uncle Judas Creek. (If that's not band-name material, I don't know what is.) And if to prove that the BWCAW really *is* the wilderness, consider this: it's home to over 10 bodies of water named "Lost Lake." Hopefully one doesn't visit Swollen Ankle Lake (also a real lake) before happening upon Lost Lake, or it could be a long trip.

Lake Itasca

Not all lakes are created equal

While all of Minnesota's lakes were created by glaciers, the state's lakes formed in two different ways. Northern Minnesota's lakes were gouged out directly by the glaciers (and the rocks they carried), and they are often deep, with relatively steep sides.

Lakes farther south were created when ice blocks fell off the retreating glaciers, pushing down the soil, forming a basin that filled in with water. These "kettle" lakes are often much shallower.

A northern pike

The deepest lake bottoms out at 240 feet

The deepest lake entirely within Minnesota is Lake Saganaga, at 240 feet.[9] Lake Superior, of course, is much deeper, 1,332 feet at its deepest. (For frame of reference, the tallest building in Minnesota, the IDS Center, is only 792 feet tall.)[10]

So how much do we fish? 87 million hours a year. And how many fish do we keep? More than 47 million

According to one estimate, if you pooled together all of the time anglers spend fishing in Minnesota, the total is something like 87 million hours.[11] That's the equivalent of 10,000 years' worth of fishing...every year. Anglers harvest (keep) somewhere around 47 million fish each year; that total includes 3.8 million walleye, 2 million northern pike and 15 million sunfish.[12]

When angling pressure is high, sometimes nature needs a little help: fish stocking

Because game fish are in such high demand, the DNR operates over a dozen fish hatcheries, which produce fish that help replenish populations in specific lakes.[13] In an average year, the DNR stocks over 310 million fish, the vast majority of which are walleye. Bass, trout and bluegill are among the other species stocked.

If you want the lakes with the most fish, head south

While northern lakes are often thought of as the prime fishing destinations, they don't actually have the most fish. Northern lakes are simply less fertile than southern lakes, so they support fewer fish than southern lakes. (This doesn't mean the fisher are bigger, though.)

Fishing isn't just a summer pastime; in winter on Lake Mille Lacs, there just might be more people ice fishing than living in the surrounding communities

In some winters, there are over 5,000 ice houses on Lake Mille Lacs.[14] Assuming one person per house, it's possible that there are more people on the lake in the winter than living around it. (For frame of reference, the largest town on the lake, Vineland, has a population of 1,000. The few other towns on the lake all clock in at triple digits.)[15] And that's the fishing population in the *winter*, when temps regularly are well below freezing.

TRIVIA TIDBIT: In the winter, some lakes even have fully functioning bars.[16] The Igloo, located on the Lake of the Woods, features indoor heating, television, hot food and booze. And better yet, you can ice fish while you eat! If that isn't odd enough, a local beer company began delivering beer to ice fishermen by drone; the FAA quickly put the kibosh on the idea.[17]

TRIVIA TIDBIT: The largest fish caught in Minnesota was a 94-pound Lake Sturgeon.[18]

A sampling of Minnesota record fish[19]

Type of Fish	Weight (lb., oz.)	Location/Year
Walleye	17 lb., 8 oz.	Saganaga Lake, 1979
Northern Pike	45 lb., 12 oz.	Basswood Lake, 1929
Largemouth Bass	8 lb., 15 oz.	Auburn Lake, 2005
Black Crappie	5 lb.	Vermilion River, 1940
Bluegill	2 lb., 13 oz.	Alice Lake, 1948
Rainbow Trout	16 lb., 6 oz.	Devil Track River, 1980
Flathead Catfish	70 lb.	St. Croix River, 1970
Lake Sturgeon (largest Minnesota fish on record)	94 lb., 4 oz.	Kettle River, 1994

The eternal question answered: who owns the lake bed?

As many lake-goers know, lake levels can vary significantly. Occasionally, this can cause the waters to recede, creating a new "beach" area. This sometimes leads to disputes among residents when the issue of lakebed ownership comes up. It's often asserted that the state owns a band of property around the lake or all of the land beneath the lake, but according to the Minnesota DNR, that's usually not true.[20] Generally speaking, the property owner's rights "go with the flow" and extend as far as the shoreline. So if you own a shoreline property and the lake is bubbling up against your back lawn, that's the extent of your property. If the water recedes and pulls back 10 feet, that 10 feet is technically yours, though there are still very strict environmental limits on what you can do with that (probably temporary) land.

We expect sunfish and northern pike, but sometimes piranhas and the occasional alligator are found in Minnesota lakes

Believe it or not, nonnative species such as piranhas and even alligators are sometimes found in Minnesota lakes.[21, 22] These are usually the result of unethical pet owners releasing their pets when they can no longer care for them. If the critters are released in summer, many subtropical and tropical critters can survive until winter arrives. For example, two anglers near Scandia were recently surprised to find an alligator floating in the water near them.[23] The alligator, a pet that had been released, was later found and shot by authorities. Another alligator from the same owner had also been released but was ultimately recaptured.

Piranhas have a (mostly undeserved) reputation, but what about *Megapiranha*?

As scary as piranhas seem, their reputation is grossly exaggerated. They actually are omnivores, which means they eat plant matter in addition to meat. While attacks are occasionally reported in their native range, they rarely cause serious injury. There is one piranha species you probably wouldn't want to swim with, though. Scientists estimate that Argentina's *Megapiranha* reached up to a meter in length.[24] Don't worry about it attacking you, though; it's been extinct for millions of years.

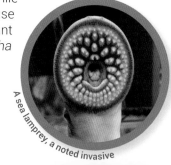
A sea lamprey, a noted invasive

Forget piranhas, our lakes are being invaded by far worse invasive species

Unfortunately, as Eurasian milfoil and the common carp make clear, winter doesn't prevent every nonnative species from establishing a population and harming lakes in Minnesota, and they do a tremendous amount of damage each year, costing the state millions.[25]

If it weren't for winter, we might have many more invasives

Our winter actually protects us from some invasive species. In warmer climates, however, many more invasive species can become established. For example, Florida's waterways are full of fish you'd probably recognize from the pet store—examples include silver dollars, oscars, and the catfish species often referred to as "sucker fish." Thankfully, piranhas have not become established in Florida, and given the threat they could pose to the state's ecosystems, they are actually illegal to own there.[26] Of course, invasives aren't just a problem in warmer regions; in some parts of the Illinois River, goldfish—yes, *those* goldfish—are one of the dominant species.[27] (Actually a species of carp, goldfish get a heck of a lot bigger when they aren't confined to a bowl.)

Pollution in the water, even in the wilderness

We often think of Minnesota's lakes as being pristine. This is especially true for lakes in areas like the Boundary Waters Canoe Area Wilderness, but unfortunately, no Minnesota lake is immune to pollution. The most common and widespread pollutant is mercury (to be specific, methylmercury), which is primarily released by coal-fired power plants, mining, and use in everyday products (such as fluorescent bulbs). Mercury pollution is distributed via the atmosphere, where it falls in Minnesota in precipitation.[28]

Beads of mercury

This means that most of the mercury in our lakes and rivers wasn't made in Minnesota; according to the Minnesota Pollution Control Agency, over 90 percent of the mercury in Minnesota came from other states (or even another country). Just as our mercury pollution comes from elsewhere, the mercury that we emit into the air doesn't stay here.

Mercury: once it's in a lake, it moves up the food chain

Once in a lake or river, the mercury is ingested or absorbed across the food chain. Once an organism has methylmercury in its system, it is usually there to stay. This causes an even bigger problem: biomagnification. When a small creature with mercury in its system is consumed by a predator, the predator absorbs that mercury. As the predator consumes other mercury-tainted prey, the amount of mercury it carries grows; this leads large-scale predators (such as large northern pike, for instance) to act as "mercury reservoirs." This is why the Minnesota DNR issues fish consumption restrictions—while a meal of fresh fish is a healthy option, too much mercury can lead to health problems. This is especially true for pregnant women or women of child-bearing age, as methylmercury can cause serious health issues for infants.

PCBs, dioxins and other pollutants

Mercury isn't the only pollutant found in Minnesota waters. Polychlorinated biphenyls, (PCBS for short) are a group of chemicals that were banned in the mid-1970s.[29] They degrade slowly in the environment and are common in Lake Superior and major rivers. Dioxins, another industrial byproduct, are also common but are usually present at low levels. Thankfully, the state tests its waterways and sets consumption guidelines. To find the guidelines for your favorite fishing hole, visit: http://www.health.state.mn.us/divs/eh/fish/eating/sitespecific.html

Lake Superior

The long-abandoned gravel cribs known as "Uncle Harvey's Mausoleum" in Duluth

The Hjørdis, a schooner, near Grand Marais

THE LARGEST FRESH-WATER LAKE IN THE WORLD BY SURFACE AREA, LAKE SUPERIOR IS ADORED BY LEGIONS OF MINNESOTANS AND HAS PLAYED A MAJOR ROLE IN MINNESOTA CULTURE AND HISTORY

The largest freshwater lake on the planet

With a surface area of just under 32,000 square miles, or about one third the area of the United Kingdom, Lake Superior is the largest freshwater lake in the world. It ranks either second or third in terms of volume, depending on your definition of a lake. The Caspian Sea is sometimes considered the largest lake in the world, as it dwarfs Lake Superior—covering a surface area of about 140,000 square miles and containing enough water to fill Lake Superior about six times over.[1] Nevertheless, as its name suggests, it is often considered a sea, since it contains saltwater (though its water is not nearly as saline as ocean water). If you ask me, any body of water that contains saltwater and is officially referred to as a "sea" isn't a lake.

At 10,000 years old, Lake Superior is considered a young pup

Even though it's an amazing 1,332 feet deep, Lake Superior is nowhere near the deepest lake in the world. That title goes to Lake Baikal, an enormous lake that is sometimes referred to as the "Pearl of Siberia" or the "Blue Eye of Siberia." Lake Baikal reaches 5,250 feet at its deepest point—almost a mile down. According to the U.S. Geological survey, it's also the oldest lake on the planet, as it's about 25 million years old. Lake Superior is quite young, geologically speaking, at only about 10,000 years of age.[2]

Lake Baikal

The deepest point in the ocean? Located beneath nearly seven miles of water

Lake Superior and Lake Baikal are certainly deep, but the oceans are much deeper. The *Titanic* sank in about two miles of water in the North Atlantic, and that's fairly shallow by oceanic standards. The deepest known portion of the ocean—the Challenger Deep—is 6.8 miles down (35,814 feet). It was named for the *H.M.S. Challenger*, a Royal Navy vessel that conducted a major scientific expedition (the Challenger Expedition) and one that led directly to advances in oceanography and many other major scientific fields. (The ill-fated U.S. Space Shuttle *Challenger* was named in honor of the Royal Navy vessel.)

The first visit to the deepest part of the ocean

The bathysphere Trieste

The Challenger Deep is part of the Mariana Trench, a narrow chasm that runs for 1,500 miles and is the boundary between two tectonic plates. The Challenger Deep was first surveyed by the two-man crew of the U.S. Navy bathysphere *Trieste* in 1960, which used about 20,000 gallons of gasoline for buoyancy. The one-of-a-kind *Trieste* is one of only two manned vessels ever to reach the Challenger Deep. (In 2012, director and explorer James Cameron reached the Challenger Deep in his submarine, the *Deepsea Challenger*.) When the *Trieste's* crew looked out the porthole, they were shocked to see what appeared to be fish swimming away. Since then, however, experts have questioned whether their observations were correct, as no fish have been observed or captured below 26,000 feet in the years since. Research in the field is ongoing, however, and it's possible specially adapted fish could be found deep in the ocean.

Duluth-Superior: The farthest inland freshwater seaports

At 2,342 miles from the Atlantic Ocean, the twin ports of Duluth-Superior are the farthest inland freshwater seaports, and they receive over 1,000 vessels each year.[3] The shipping season is usually open for about nine months, closing in January and reopening in March. To reach Duluth and Superior, ships must traverse the St. Lawrence Seaway, an engineering marvel that allows ocean-going ships to travel through all of the Great Lakes. Starting in the St. Lawrence River (which connects to the Gulf of St. Lawrence on the Atlantic), there is a series of locks near Montreal that allows ships to travel through the St. Lawrence River, which eventually reaches Lake Ontario.[4] From there, the ships traverse the smallest Great Lake, before reaching another series of locks and

The famed Aerial Lift Bridge in Duluth

the Welland Canal, a man-made canal that bypasses Niagara Falls. Ships proceed through Lake Erie, into Lake Huron, eventually leading to Sault St. Marie, Michigan, where ships must pass through the Soo Locks to reach Lake Superior.

The St. Lawrence Seaway: the "greatest construction show on Earth"

Creating the Seaway was a daunting task, as it involved moving over 200 million cubic yards of earth and more concrete than was used in the Hoover Dam.[5, 6, 7] In all, 22,000 people worked on the project. Built over the course of four years, the Seaway also dramatically altered the landscape and the lives of thousands of area residents. A number of dams were constructed to control lake levels and provide power. These dams flooded over 100 square miles of land, and the affected Canadian communities—many of which were occupied by indigenous peoples—were resettled in purpose-built "new towns."[8]

Ship locks are gravity-powered!

Locks are the heart of the St. Lawrence Seaway System, and despite all of the engineering that went into creating the massive system, locks are surprisingly simple devices. Used to raise or lower a ship to a different water level, locks consist of a step-like system of pools that can be sealed off by gates. When a ship enters a lock, a valve is opened so water can flow into (or out of) the lock. This either raises or lowers the water level—and the ship. Once the correct level is reached, the valve is closed, and the other gate is opened so the ship can leave the lock. Amazingly, the locks of the St. Lawrence Seaway don't require pumps. The water flows into and out of the locks because of gravity.[9] The difference in elevation between Lake Ontario and Lake Superior is 328 feet, the height of a thirty-story building.

> **TRIVIA TIDBIT:** It takes 24 million gallons of water to fill one lock; that's enough for 36 Olympic-sized swimming pools; a body of water of that size would exceed 10 acres, and in Minnesota it'd likely be considered a small lake.[10, 11]

The Paul R. Tregurtha passing through a lock

Some ships are just too big to fit through the locks: the maximum size? 740 feet long

Even though locks of the St. Lawrence Seaway are huge—766 feet long—some ships are simply too big to fit in the locks. The maximum size a ship can be and still fit in the locks is known as "Seawaymax"; Seawaymax ships can't exceed 740 feet in length.[12] This restriction affects oceangoing ships and lake freighters alike, which means that the ships in excess of 740 feet are confined to life on the "upper" four Great Lakes forever. Because some vessels can venture onto the open ocean, each type of vessel has its own nickname; vessels that remain solely on the lakes are called lake freighters or "lakers"; oceangoing vessels are called "salties."

There are thirteen lakers over 1,000 feet on the Great Lakes

Despite the size restrictions of the locks, there are many lake freighters that are too large to pass through them. In fact, 13 lakers exceed 1,000 feet—the largest, the *Paul R. Tregurtha* is 1,013 feet, 6 inches long. For frame of reference, the *Titanic*—no small ship—was 883 feet long, so the 1,000-footers are considerably longer than even that famous ill-fated vessel.[13]

An ore boat at the Soo Locks

The RMS Titanic

A 1,000-footer carries enough wheat to make bread for eight million people . . . for a month

The best way to learn how big these ships really are is to wrap your head around how much they can carry. It's a staggering amount. According to the corporation responsible for managing the seaway, a "1,000-foot-long ship from the Great Lakes carries enough iron ore to operate a steel mill for more than four days or enough wheat to make bread for everyone in New York City for a month."[14]

There were once pirates on the Great Lakes

When you think of pirates, you probably think of frigates bristling with cannons plying the waters of the Caribbean, but piracy also occurred on the Great Lakes. Of course, the pirates on the Great Lakes were not the flawed-but-admirable figures like Disney's Captain Jack Sparrow. Just as their Caribbean counterparts were often murderers and slavers, the Great Lakes pirates were often little more than thieves, and the primary loot that they were after was hardly the stuff of the Spanish Treasure Fleet. On the contrary, the pirates of the Great Lakes often raided ships carrying cargo with a distinctively Northwoods flair, especially timber and venison.

"Roaring" Dan Seavey: the most infamous pirate on the Great Lakes

Perhaps the most famous pirate of the Great Lakes was "Roaring" Dan Seavey, an almost legendary figure best known for inciting a mutiny on a merchant vessel, *the Nellie Johnson* and then leading the U.S. cutter *Tuscarora* on a week-long chase through Lake Michigan.[15] As you might expect, this tale was immediately embellished by national newspapers, and the existing accounts differ wildly about the details. The *New York Times* reported that Seavey was taken into custody after a shot was literally fired over his ship's bow, but this doesn't actually seem to be the case, as the *Tuscarora's* captain's log indicates that Seavey simply surrendered and was arrested by the U.S. Marshal on board.[16, 17] Seavey later escaped indictment thanks to a favorable grand jury.

"Moon Cussing": a shady tactic to wreck ships–and steal their cargo

Moon cussing was a tactic that Dan Seavey was no doubt familiar with. "Moon cussers" created fake navigational lights or extinguished existing ones, causing ships to be run aground on rocks or shoals. The pirates would then salvage the cargo from the disabled ships. This technique gets its name because the would-be wreck scavengers "cuss the moon" when its light prevents them from illegally salvaging a wreck in secret.[18]

"Roaring" Dan Seavey

TRIVIA TIDBIT: The Great Lakes Distillery even named one of their rum varieties after "Roaring Dan Seavey." They've also created a special drink, the "Moon Cusser" in his honor. Appropriately enough, it is served on the rocks.[19]

Timber pirates on lakes and rivers

Lumberjacks in Effie, Minnesota

Minnesota and the Great Lakes area were also home to the timber pirates of the 1850s, who did far more damage to the region than Dan Seavey. As their name suggests, they trafficked in timber, which they illegally harvested on government and private land, and the timber was then shipped via the Great Lakes to be sold elsewhere. As much of the region's great unspoiled forests were wholly unattended, this led to huge swaths of land being illegally deforested.[20] This ravaged the environment, led to future forest fires and caused the loss of millions of dollars' worth of lumber.

Warships once patrolled the Great Lakes to fight piracy and smuggling

The USS Michigan

Timber piracy[21] got so bad that the U.S. Navy sent a warship—the USS *Michigan*—to patrol the Great Lakes and break up the smuggling operations.[22] The *Michigan* was the Navy's first iron-hulled warship, and she spent her entire career patrolling the Great Lakes. The tactic helped somewhat, but timber piracy—spurred by the major lumber barons—continued until the vast majority of the native forests was essentially clear-cut.

TRIVIA TIDBIT: Oddly, when the *Michigan* was first launched, she got stuck halfway down the launching ramp.[23] After darkness fell, the workers went home. When they came back the next day, the ship was found floating undamaged off the coast.

On rare occasions, the Great Lakes freeze over entirely

The shipping season ends when the ice cover becomes too prominent. While the U.S. Coast Guard operates a fleet of ice-breakers that create shipping lanes, the shipping season doesn't

usually begin again until late March. Occasionally, Superior freezes over almost entirely. This is relatively rare and has occurred only a few times since the 1990s.[24] (In even rarer winters, all the other Great Lakes freeze over as well.) According to the National Atmospheric and Oceanic Administration, the average Great Lakes ice cover is about 50 percent.[25]

Lake Superior covered in ice

> **TRIVIA TIDBIT:** When the Big Lake does freeze over, there are certain benefits. For example, towns like Bayfield, Wisconsin, often see huge tourism booms thanks to their famous sea caves, which are usually inaccessible. During the last big freeze, Bayfield saw more than 35,000 people visit its ice caves.[26]

Surf's up: surfing is a popular pastime on the Great Lakes, especially in November

While Superior's waves have sunk many vessels, there are some surprising beneficiaries of Superior's big waves: surfers. Yes, you read that correctly—surfing has become a popular activity for a die-hard group on the Great Lakes. Especially popular during the ice-free and stormy months of October and November, surfing the lakes requires much of the same equipment as surfing elsewhere—though would-be surfers need an appropriate wetsuit for the winter months. That doesn't mean you won't get cold, however. Surfers on the Great Lakes often end their day with icicles hanging from their facemasks.

> **TRIVIA TIDBIT:** The surfing scene has gotten so popular that the Chicago area actually boasts a pair of surf shops that cater to the burgeoning surfing crowd in the region. So if you need a surfboard, look up either of the Third Coast Surf Shop stores.[27] (Sadly, there is no Lake Superior-oriented surf shop in Minnesota yet.)

Storms on the Great Lakes can be as bad as on the open ocean

Even though Lake Superior and the Great Lakes may not rival the open oceans in terms of size or depth, mariners report that the storms that occur on the Great Lakes can be as bad as those on the ocean—and often harder to navigate. Many of the worst storms occur in the fall

(November is particularly infamous), as the conditions are often perfect for storm formation. Large, low-pressure systems (cold air) descend from the north and mix with warmer, humid air that originates from the Gulf of Mexico. By itself, this is a recipe for trouble, but the Great Lakes themselves provide more energy to the storms, as the lakes tend to cool rather slowly and retain some of summer's heat well into fall. The lakes are therefore much warmer than the air that is present in the low-pressure systems arriving from the north. This often results in massive storms.

A small number of safe harbors and suddenly shallow waters make for treacherous sailing

Another problem for sailors on the Great Lakes is that there's less room to maneuver than on the open ocean. The lakes are quite shallow compared to the ocean, and there are often many hazards along the way, including islands, reefs and shoals. And on many parts of the lake (Minnesota's North Shore for instance), there are relatively few safe harbors. In many places, any sort of harbor is absent altogether, and the waves sometimes lead straight into sheer cliffs. Once a vessel is up against a cliff or a reef, it gets battered to pieces by the relentless surf.

Split Rock Lighthouse

On the Great Lakes, the waves don't stop coming

Compared to ocean waves, the waves on the Great Lakes are generally smaller, but that doesn't mean their waters are much safer.[28] On the Great Lakes, there is generally less time between waves. On the ocean, a wave might hit every 15 seconds or so, whereas on the Great Lakes, one might hit every four or five seconds. While this example is an obvious generalization, you get the point. On the Great Lakes, a never-ending assault of relatively small waves can make a trip very uncomfortable and, sometimes, potentially dangerous.[29]

Palisade Head

Rogue waves on the ocean—and perhaps on Superior

For generations, sailors have often referred to "rogue waves," massive individual waves (or a set of huge waves) that were much larger than the rest of the waves at a given time. These waves were often reputed to be huge—sometimes 100 feet tall—and they were responsible for sinking vessels, which were simply overcome. Until recently, rogue waves were considered part of sailors' lore, but scientists have since recorded instances of positively humongous waves; in 2000, the RRS *Discovery* was hit by a *95-foot-tall* wave.[30] The ship survived, and the data it collected helped confirm the existence of rogue waves. As it turns out, researchers have found that freak waves aren't particularly rare—satellite observations of the open ocean indicate that they happen much more than one would think.[31] Thankfully, rogue waves are very short-lived, so very few vessels are actually affected. A similar phenomenon is said to occur on the Great Lakes. Referred to as the "Three Sisters" it occurs when three large waves strike in quick succession. The existence of the "Three Sisters" has yet to be confirmed by scientific instruments, but given the many reports by experienced captains, it certainly seems likely that the Great Lakes have rogue waves as well.

A large wave astern of a NOAA ship in New England

A Sampling of Lake Superior Shipwrecks

A squall line on Superior

A Lake Superior wreck

SHIPWRECKS DON'T JUST HAPPEN ON THE OCEAN. LAKE SUPERIOR IS HOME TO HUNDREDS OF WRECKS, INCLUDING SOME OF THE MOST FAMOUS IN U.S. HISTORY

Not even natural harbors are necessarily safe

In autumn, weather conditions often conspire to drive vessels on Lake Superior directly toward hazards. This can even make ports and natural harbors dangerous places.[1] In 1872, a pair of storms ravaged the original Duluth Port, which was relatively unprotected. This led to the construction of the current port behind the protection of Minnesota Point.[2]

Over 6,000 ships have sunk in the Great Lakes, with a total of perhaps 30,000 sailors lost

All told, thousands of ships have gone down since the seventeenth century. According to one estimate, more than 6,000 ships have sunk in the Great Lakes, perhaps 550 of which have gone down in Lake Superior.[3] Minnesota's North Shore alone has nearly 50 wrecks.[4] In all, something like 30,000 people have died in wrecks on the Great Lakes.

Some areas are known as the Graveyards of Lake Superior

From the *Mataafa* to the *Edmund Fitzgerald*, some of the most infamous disasters in maritime history occurred on Lake Superior. Not surprisingly, many of these wrecks are clustered around the same geographical areas. Often referred to as the Graveyards of Lake Superior, many shipwrecks on Lake Superior have occurred near Isle Royale, Whitefish Point, Whitefish Bay and the Keweenaw Peninsula.[5] While these locales are scattered across the lake, they have many similarities: All are positively littered with reefs, shoals and tremendous variations in depth. These hazards are also often downwind of the shipping lanes, so when bad weather arises, ships are pushed toward them, making an already dangerous situation worse.

Isle Royale

TRIVIA TIDBIT: How hazardous can navigation be on the lakes? Just outside the Harlem Reef, on the southern shore of Isle Royale on Lake Superior, the water is 125 feet deep.[6] A few hundred feet away, it's two feet deep. Not surprisingly, a wreck is located near the reef.

Some ships simply vanished

When you read through the accounts of the shipwrecks of Lake Superior, it's surprising to learn how little we know about what happened to many ships. This is especially true in the era before the introduction of the telegraph. Some ships simply vanished, and their locations and the causes of their sinkings remain mysteries. Modern technology doesn't always help; the *Edmund Fitzgerald* had modern technology but never issued a distress call. The last transmission simply stated, "We are holding our own." While her wreck has been found, the cause of the *Fitzgerald's* sinking has been hotly debated since she sank.

A ship's engine room telegraph

A chart of Harlem Reef

In the early days, 20 vessels lost in a season was routine

The statistics from the early 1900s are sobering and give an idea of just how dangerous the lakes are. It wasn't uncommon for 20 vessels (or many more!) to be lost on the lakes each season, resulting in the loss of hundreds of lives.

The death toll at the turn of the century in Great Lakes shipping[7]

1908: 220
1909: 121
1910: 45
1911: 51
1912: 33
1913: 253 (The White Hurricane, pg. 67)
1914: 54
1915: 863*
1916: 73
1917-1919: 0 aboard bulk freighters, although deaths occurred on other ships

*844 died in the Eastland Disaster (pg. 66), which took place on the Chicago River. Nineteen deaths occurred on the Great Lakes proper.

TRIVIA TIDBIT: Oddly, the worst shipwreck involving a Great Lakes vessel didn't even happen on the Great Lakes. The SS *Eastland* was a passenger ship that was docked in the Chicago River and taking on passengers for a tour.[8] The ship quickly became unbalanced after hundreds of passengers boarded in only a few minutes, and it developed a list. The crew made attempts to correct it, but these failed, and soon the ship capsized, throwing hundreds of people into the water and crushing many more. In the end, 844 people died. Ironically, the ship may have capsized in part because of lifeboats that had been recently installed. Mandated after the loss of the *Titanic*, their added weight may have made the ship more top-heavy.[9]

The lake really doesn't give up her dead

In Gordon Lightfoot's song "Wreck of the Edmund Fitzgerald" he famously repeats an old line about Lake Superior: She never gives up her dead.[10] As it turns out, it's true. The lake's water is so cold that it inhibits bacterial growth, preventing the bodies from floating to the surface. So in many cases, sailors that are lost aboard a ship on the Great Lakes are never seen again.

The SS *Eastland*

A sampling of Lake Superior shipwrecks

Vessel	Lives Lost	Month/Year	Location
W.W. Arnold[11]	17	November 1869	Near Whitefish Point
Manistee[12]	~20	November 1883	Michigan coast
Scotia[13]	None	October 1884	Keweenaw Peninsula
Algona[14]	45-47	November 1885	Isle Royale
Western Reserve[15]	26	August 1892	Near Whitefish Point
Henry B. Smith[16]	25	November 1913	Near Marquette, MI
Inkerman and Cerisolles	76	November 1918	Keweenaw Point
Henry Steinbrenner[17]	17	May 1953	Isle Royale
Edmund Fitzgerald	29	November 1975	Near Whitefish Point

Storms and shipwrecks

While many ill-fated Great Lakes vessels sank because of steam-boiler explosions, fires or collisions, Lake Superior's notorious storms have claimed their fair share. In the era before reliable weather forecasting, massive storms often caught vessels unaware, and the worst of those storms were as bad as storms seen on the ocean. In fact, hurricane-force winds aren't unheard of; in the infamous Storm of 1913—also known as the White Hurricane—a computer simulation indicates that gusts of hurricane-force winds were present on Lake Superior for 20 hours.[18] Gusts were estimated at 80 miles per hour and may have even topped 100 miles per hour, with waves reaching 36 feet high. Nine Great Lakes vessels were sunk in the storm, with 200 people killed in all. On Lake Superior alone, two ships and 43 sailors were lost.[19]

Hurricanes on the ocean are named; so are the worst storms on the Great Lakes

The Great Lakes' storms share something else in common with hurricanes: The worst storms are often named. Sailors refer to the Mataafa Storm of 1905, the White Hurricane of 1913, the

Armistice Day Storm of 1940 and more recently the "Chiclone" of 2010, which produced waves of over 20 feet on Lake Superior.[20]

Without the United States Lifesaving Service, things would have been much worse

Shocked by the horrific losses on the Great Lakes and elsewhere, the federal government was spurred into action and created a number of organizations to improve safety on the lakes. This included the United States Lighthouse Service, which built lighthouses on the Great Lakes, and the United States Lifesaving Service, which built lifesaving stations with crews who rushed into the worst storms to assist ailing vessels. (Both organizations would eventually be merged into the U.S. Coast Guard.) The Lighthouse Service even operated "lightships" where lighthouses were impossible to build. These improvements were a piecemeal process, but thanks to advances in shipbuilding, additional lighthouses and enhanced navigational markers, shipping on the Great Lakes became much safer. At the turn of the twentieth century, each shipping season averaged dozens of deaths and many ships lost; in the twenty-first century, shipwrecks and deaths are now incredibly rare.

Minnesota's seven lighthouses

There are seven active lighthouses in Minnesota, in addition to a number of light towers.[21] Many of the state's lighthouses have been preserved. Split Rock Lighthouse is now one of the most popular state parks in Minnesota, and the Two Harbors Lighthouse is now home to a bed and breakfast (in addition to a museum).[22]

> **TRIVIA TIDBIT:** There is even a pair of lighthouses on the Mississippi River.[23] There's one at Boom Island and one on Lake Pepin, where the river is about a mile across.

Shipwreck hunting and wreck diving: two popular pastimes on the North Shore

Because of the many wrecks that simply vanished, shipwreck hunting is alive and well on the

Great Lakes, and long-forgotten wrecks continue to be discovered.[24] When wrecks are discovered, they are often found in good condition, thanks to the lake's temperature—nearly always just about 39 degrees—and its fresh water, which does less damage to iron than saltwater. This makes the more-accessible shipwrecks popular with scuba divers. Unfortunately, unscrupulous divers have looted the most-accessible wrecks—many of which still contained human remains—so the U.S. Congress passed the Abandoned Shipwreck Act in 1987, which made all shipwrecks the property of their respective state and banned the collection of artifacts without permission.[25] This "leave no trace" ethos has caught on among divers, and many of Minnesota's diveable wrecks are still in good condition.

A shipwreck on Michigan's Lake Superior coast

The only treasure ship of the Great Lakes

Most Great Lakes vessels carry fairly pedestrian cargo—iron ore, coal or grain—but one Lake Superior vessel sank bearing a cargo of silver ore. The *Comet* sunk off Whitefish Bay in 1875 after colliding with another vessel, and while the wreck has been discovered, the 70 tons of ore remain unaccounted for, as they likely mixed in with the sediment.[26]

> **TRIVIA TIDBIT:** Treasure fleets did exist elsewhere. The fabled Spanish treasure fleets sailed from Florida and the Caribbean carrying their plunder from the New World back to Spain. In 1715, 11 silver-bearing ships were lost off the eastern coast of Florida, and artifacts occasionally still wash up on beaches in southeastern Florida.

Shipwrecks: not a thing of the past

Even though technology has improved, shipwrecks and accidents still happen on the Great Lakes. Sometimes, they happen to even the most modern of vessels. In fact, in 2012 the 1,013-foot long *Paul R. Tregurtha* ran aground in the St. Marys River due to pilot error, blocking an entire shipping lane for a day.[27] The ship is the current "Queen of the Lake"—the largest ship on the Great Lakes—and it was put out of action for an entire month because of the damage caused by the accident. Thankfully, no one was hurt, and the ship is still in service.

TRIVIA TIDBIT: The Minnesota DNR advises boaters always to bring along an AM radio to monitor weather reports; they note that even if one can't get a station to come in, you can tell a storm is coming because of increased "crashes" of static on AM radio.[28] This static is caused by lightning strikes, which produce radio waves in addition to visible light.

TRIVIA TIDBIT: Every few summers in July, Duluth's Tall Ships Festival welcomes a number of large sailing vessels to the harbor. One of the previous guests of honor was the *Bounty*, a reconstruction of the *H.M.S. Bounty* that was built in 1960 for use in the film *Mutiny on the Bounty*. That ship would eventually meet its demise in Superstorm Sandy. Despite widespread weather reports about the approach of Superstorm Sandy, its captain inexplicably led the vessel out to sea, where it quickly began taking on water.[29] The weather conditions at the time were horrendous—winds were topping 50-60 knots (with gusts much higher), and seas were over 20 feet high. Eventually, the captain contacted the Coast Guard, but by then it was too late, and the crew had to abandon ship. A Coast Guard plane was dispatched to monitor the situation, and when one of the Coast Guard crew on the plane was asked what he saw, he replied, "I see a pirate ship in the middle of a hurricane!" Sadly, the captain and one crew member died; the Coast Guard saved the rest of the crew, and in a scathing report, the *Bounty's* captain was faulted for going out to sea to begin with.

The Bounty sinking

The first wreck on Superior: The schooner *Madeline* in 1838

Because historical records during the fur trade and prior to settlement are spotty, it's not clear when the first shipwreck occurred on Lake Superior, but the schooner *Madeline* likely takes the dubious prize.[30, 31] It sunk during a storm after it was pushed into ice floes near the Knife River. Unfortunately, given its final resting place, most of the wreckage is presumably buried under sediment.

> **TRIVIA TIDBIT:** Minnesota's greatest maritime disaster happened on Lake Pepin, which is actually part of the Mississippi River.[32] Almost a hundred people died when the *Sea Wing* capsized.

The Mataafa Wreck

Duluth North Pier Light

The *Mataafa*: front row seat to a disaster

Not all shipwrecks happen far from shore. Sometimes, they happen in plain sight. During a late November storm in 1905, the *Mataafa* began steaming out of the harbor while towing a barge, only to quickly turn around after encountering a huge storm. After cutting the tow line and instructing the barge to anchor, the *Mataafa* attempted to re-enter the harbor, but a huge swell of water smashed the ship into a pier; eventually the ship broke into three pieces. The captain called for help on a megaphone, but the lifesaving crews were already occupied with another wreck elsewhere, and the waters were too treacherous once help actually arrived. By the time rescuers made it aboard, all nine of the crew members in the stern of the ship were dead. The crew[33] had suffered and died just several hundred feet from shore and in earshot of thousands. Many of the bodies had to be chipped out of the ice.

The SS *Henry Steinbrenner*

By the 1950s, advances in weather forecasting, communications technology and shipbuilding had made shipping on the Great Lakes much safer. Nonetheless, there were a number of wrecks throughout the Great Lakes in the 1950s and 1960s, making it clear that the Great Lakes are an inherently dangerous place. Prior to the sinking of the *Edmund Fitzgerald*, the SS *Henry Steinbrenner* was perhaps one of Lake Superior's most infamous cautionary tales. Named in honor of the shipping magnate Henry Steinbrenner, the SS *Henry Steinbrenner* began taking on water on May 11, 1953, during a hurricane-strength storm near Isle Royale; thankfully, 13 members of its crew were saved, though 17 were lost.[34]

> **TRIVIA TIDBIT:** As for the ship itself, if its last name sounds familiar, it should; Henry Steinbrenner's son, George, was the famous (infamous?) owner of the New York Yankees.

The *Edmund Fitzgerald:* the most famous wreck on the Great Lakes

By the 1970s, major shipwrecks were almost unheard of on the Great Lakes, but on November 10, 1975, Lake Superior proved that her raw power was still a force to contend with, as the *Edmund Fitzgerald* sank with all hands lost.[35] The ship, which was being battered by a hurricane-force storm and 25-foot seas, began taking on water. The *Fitzgerald* was in radio contact with the nearby *Arthur M. Anderson*, which was attempting to catch up to it and guide it to safety. Unfortunately, the weather was ravaging the *Fitzgerald*; it got so bad that it kept disappearing and reappearing from radar. This occurred because the waves were so large that they were actually getting in the way of the radar's beams.[36] The last communication from the *Fitzgerald* ended with its captain saying, "We are holding our own." Soon thereafter, the *Anderson's* crew noted that the *Fitzgerald* wasn't visible on radar and not responding to radio. All 29 of the *Fitzgerald's* crew went down with the ship. The wreck was soon located in 530 feet of water; the ship had split into two pieces.

The Edmund Fitzgerald

Rogue waves: a potential cause of the sinking?

Recently, it has been claimed that the *Fitzgerald* succumbed to a rogue wave. The *Arthur M. Anderson*, the last ship to communicate with the *Fitz*, reported that it was struck by a pair of waves in excess of 30 feet.[37] Bernie Cooper, the captain of the *Anderson*, later said, "I think those were the two that sent [the *Fitzgerald*] under." However the *Fitzgerald* sank, the loss lingers, and memorial services are still held on the date of the sinking.[38] Split Rock Lighthouse lights its beacon, and the names of the crew are read aloud; at the Great Lakes Shipwreck Museum, the *Fitzgerald's* bell, which was recovered from the ship, sounds 30 times, once for each of the 29 crew member lost, and once for the thousands of other sailors lost on the Great Lakes. Thankfully, no lake freighters have gone down since the *Fitzgerald* in 1975.

Talk about eerie: the Edmund Fitzgerald Storm, Part II

Twenty-three years to the day of the sinking of the *Edmund Fitzgerald*, another storm raged on the Great Lakes.[39] Traveling along almost the exact same path as the storm that sank the *Fitzgerald*, it carried comparable winds and produced huge waves. Thankfully, no ships were lost in that storm.

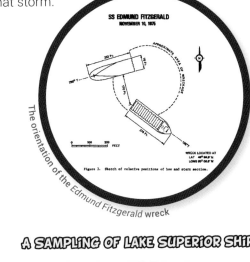

The Edmund Fitzgerald Storm, Part II

The orientation of the Edmund Fitzgerald wreck

The mill disaster, courtesy of the General Mills Archives

Minnesota Disasters

FROM ASTEROID IMPACTS TO MILL EXPLOSIONS, MINNESOTA HAS ENDURED ITS FAIR SHARE OF DISASTERS, AND EACH HAS LEFT AN IMPORTANT MARK ON MINNESOTA

A headline from the Mill Disaster of 1878

An iron-lung-polio was once a common threat in Minnesota

Asteroid Strike

An asteroid ravaged the BWCAW 1.8 billion years ago

Located near the Boundary Waters Canoe Area Wilderness, Gunflint Lodge is a Minnesota destination. It's also known for its curious fireplace; for years, people—especially geologists!—wondered about the strange stones that had been used in its fireplace. As it turns out, those stones were the result of an impact event that struck far-off Sudbury, Ontario, some 480 miles away. You might wonder: If it's so far away, how could the area possibly have been affected? Well, the impactor is estimated to have been ten miles in diameter; for frame of reference, that's *much* larger than the one that likely killed the dinosaurs. According to the Minnesota Geological Survey, the impact would have had a devastating impact over thousands of miles.[1] At Gunflint Lake, here is what the impact may have been like:

An artist's impression of a major impact

After about 13 seconds, the fireball—traveling over 130,000 miles per hour, reaches the lake—causing third-degree burns and starting trees on fire. After two to three minutes, an earthquake clocking in at 10.2 on the Richter scale hits, collapsing any structures. For reference, the strongest recorded earthquake was 9.5, in Chile—and it's important to note that the Richter scale is logarithmic. This means that each number on the scale is much more powerful than the previous one. To be exact, the earthquake created by the Sudbury impact was 5.623 times stronger (in terms of energy release) than the strongest earthquake ever recorded.[2]

And that's only half of it. If you survived the earthquake (unlikely!) you'd have to survive the "one to three meters" of ejecta that would blanket the area after five to ten minutes. After that, it would get a bit windy. The air blast would arrive 40 minutes later and pack winds of 1,400 miles per hour.

The Spanish Flu and Polio

The Spanish Flu of 1918 and the worst pandemic in history

What we call the Spanish Flu actually originated in rural Kansas; U.S. Army soldiers were first infected, and as they were being mobilized to enter the war, they brought the flu with them to Europe.[1] Perversely, the afflicted were often young and healthy, and they died relatively quickly. The absolutely staggering thing about this flu is how many people were killed—anywhere from 50 to 100 million people globally—probably more than any other pandemic in history.[2] To put that into perspective, over the course of four years, World War I killed something like 16 million people. The flu killed tens of millions more in just two years.

Influenza patients being treated

Minnesota was hit hard: in the worst month of the flu in Minnesota, 3,260 people died[3]

The pandemic lasted two years globally, but it only lasted about seven months in Minnesota. In that time, 10,000 Minnesotans died. Just how bad was the flu in the U.S.? An estimated 550,000 people died, nearly five times more than the number of U.S. soldiers killed in World War I.[4,5]

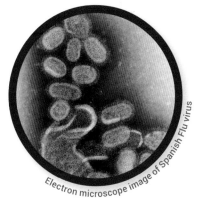

Electron microscope image of Spanish Flu virus

Despite its carnage, the Spanish Flu is often considered a forgotten disaster

In a certain respect, this actually makes sense. Given the unprecedented horror of mechanized warfare and the slaughter of the First World War—19,240 British soldiers were killed on the first day of the Battle of the Somme alone—the population was already shell-shocked (a term that itself stems from the war). After all, they didn't call the survivors "the Lost Generation" for nothing. The flu just made an already miserable situation worse.

Yet another reason to get vaccinated: the 1946 Minnesota State Fair was canceled because of a polio outbreak

Long eradicated in the U.S., polio doesn't mean much for many of us. Nonetheless, in the 1940s and the 1950s, polio epidemics were positively terrifying for parents because the disease primarily afflicts children.[6] Caused by a virus that lives amid sewage, polio outbreaks primarily occurred in summer when children swam in pools and other contaminated bodies of water. Some years were worse than others; in bad years, society would virtually shut down. The outbreak of 1946 is a prime example of this. In Minnesota, there were 2,881 cases and 226 deaths, and some survivors were left entirely or partially paralyzed.[7] In an attempt to prevent the spread of the disease, the Minnesota State Fair was canceled. Schools were also closed and city life essentially shut down.

1952: the worst polio outbreak in Minnesota history

The 1946 polio outbreak was bad, but the 1952 outbreak was far worse. With 4,131 cases and 220 deaths, Minnesota was the epicenter of the national outbreak.[8] Perversely, this outbreak occurred just a few years before the widespread adoption of the first reliable polio vaccine. In the '40s and '50s, polio was a menace; a decade after the introduction of the vaccine, deaths were almost unheard of. Polio was eradicated in the U.S. by 1979.

> **TRIVIA TIDBIT:** The March of Dimes was originally formed to defeat polio. Today, a single dose of vaccine costs about a dime.[9]

Smallpox and Other Diseases
A smallpox epidemic in the Midwest ravaged American Indian tribes from 1775 to 1782

Electron microscope image of smallpox virus

Already facing serious stresses due to scant resources, competition with other tribes and the sudden incursion of Europeans, American Indian tribes in Minnesota were absolutely devastated by the introduction of smallpox and other diseases from Europe. While there were many localized outbreaks, an epidemic starting in 1775 and lasting to 1782 was especially brutal. More sedentary tribes (such as the Mandan, Hidatsa and Arikara populations of the western Great Plains) were devastated, losing perhaps 70 to 80 percent of their populations.[1] Minnesota's more mobile populations (such as the Dakota and the Ojibwe) probably fared somewhat better, but they still lost a significant percentage of their populations.[2]

Prior to vaccination, inoculation–giving oneself a moderate infection–was the primary way to prevent smallpox

Europeans had much to fear from smallpox as well. The threat was so great—the death toll was usually around 30 percent—that Europeans resorted to inoculation (also known as variolation). The process involved taking a dried pustule from an infected smallpox victim and inserting it beneath a person's skin. The person would then develop the disease and contract the illness—but it was usually an attenuated (weakened) form, and once they recovered, they were immune to the disease. Inoculation was not without its risks, however: a small percentage (two to three percent) died from the disease, and the newly inoculated were incapacitated for roughly a month, during which time they could transmit it to others, sparking fresh outbreaks.[3] And as you might expect, the process could also inadvertently transmit other serious diseases, including tuberculosis and syphilis.

Inoculation may have helped George Washington win the Revolutionary War[4]

Still, inoculation was often worth the risks. After initially banning the procedure—which could incapacitate a large amount of troops in a short time—George Washington famously had new soldiers inoculated against smallpox.[5] Given that disease was often as large a threat—or a greater one—than enemy soldiers, this type of inoculation just might have helped the Colonies win their independence.[6]

Crossing the Delaware by Emanuel Leutze

Compulsory smallpox vaccination was repealed in 1903, leading to the smallpox epidemic of 1924-1925

Eventually, thanks largely to the work of Edward Jenner (the creator of the smallpox vaccine), a safe and effective smallpox vaccine was developed in 1800 based on the similar (but harmless) cowpox virus. Unfortunately, even though the vaccine had been around for over a century, compulsory vaccination was illegal in Minnesota in the 1920s (it had been legal previously).[7] In January of 1924, an unvaccinated man died of smallpox, and by June, the disease was spreading in the Twin Cities, where it eventually infected thousands, killing 504. A mass-vaccination program during the outbreak helped prevent additional cases.

Oregon Trail diseases struck Minnesota: typhoid, diphtheria and cholera[8]

A number of other diseases have reached epidemic status in Minnesota, and if you've ever played the game *Oregon Trail*, many of them are familiar. Typhoid and cholera are both bacterial infections and occur when victims ingest water from contaminated sources. Prior to the development of modern sanitation and water treatment, the diseases were a common threat in Minnesota, and they often reached epidemic proportions. Typhoid epidemics occurred in 1897, and also in 1910, when 700 died.[9,10] Cholera was another threat and over five pandemics have affected the U.S., including four that had some effect on Minnesota.[11,12] Diphtheria, which is caused by a virus, also struck Minnesota on several occasions, though quarantining victims (and an eventual vaccine) have since eliminated the threat.[13]

Mine Disasters and Other Catastrophes

Forty-one miners died in the worst mine disaster in Minnesota history

A high-quality iron ore and manganese mine, the Milford Mine is infamous as the site of the worst mining disaster in Minnesota history.[1] Unlike the open-pit iron mines on the Mesabi range today, the Milford Mine was an underground mine, and miners tunneled through rock to obtain ore. The mine, which was located in Crosby and situated in between two lakes and near a bog, was constantly wet, and pumps were in operation to keep it from flooding. Eventually the mine tunnel began approaching the bog, and on February 5, 1924, disaster struck. The bog caved in, and water poured in, flooding the mine, drowning 41 men. Seven lucky miners managed to escape, thanks to a number of acts of heroism, including a miner who stayed at his post to signal a warning to other miners rather than flee for his life. Over the following months, the adjacent lake was drained entirely, and all of the bodies were painstakingly removed and buried, the last being laid to rest nine months after the disaster.[2]

While the Milford Mine disaster was the worst in state history, it wasn't the only one; given the dangerous conditions and equipment, fatal accidents and serious injuries were hardly uncommon. Two smaller disasters occurred at Silver Mine and the Norman Mine in Virginia and at Ely's Sibley Shaft No. 9.[3]

Plagues of locusts once struck Minnesota (no, really!)

Given their prevalence in Exodus, plagues of locusts are often associated with the Old Testament, not Minnesota. Nonetheless, in the late 1870s, Minnesota's crops were under literal attack.[4] On four different occasions, Rocky Mountain Locusts swarmed into the state, damaging or outright devouring much of the state's crops. In the first wave, only a handful of counties were affected, but soon thereafter, locusts ruined crops in many more counties.

A Rocky Mountain Locust

Laura Ingalls Wilder and locusts

Of course, many Minnesotans are familiar with the state's locust problem thanks to famed author Laura Ingalls Wilder. In 1874, Wilder and her family moved to Walnut Grove, Minnesota, when Wilder was seven. The girl grew up as a pioneer and a farmer. She later wrote about her family's experiences in a series of nine *Little House* books. (The first wasn't published until Ingalls was 65 years old!) In her fourth book, *On the Banks of Plum Creek*, she detailed the locust plague, although she referred to them as grasshoppers. Wilder's popular series of books later inspired the timeless television series *Little House on the Prairie*.

Things got so bad that Governor John Pillsbury dedicated a specific day of "Fasting, Prayer and Humiliation" in an attempt to rid the state of locusts

Governor John S. Pillsbury

At first, the state enacted a number of laws to combat the locusts. A bounty system was established that offered cash for grasshopper eggs or live specimens. When the bounty system didn't prove popular, a grasshopper draft was established that mandated that males between ages 21 and 60 hunt for grasshoppers one day a week for five weeks. Eventually, the Governor declared April 26, 1877, a day of "Fasting, Prayer and Humiliation" in an attempt to spur divine intervention that would prevent the spring crop of grasshoppers from hatching.[5] The grasshopper eggs did emerge, but they quickly left the state. Oddly, the species that caused the grasshopper plagues has since gone extinct.

Plane Crashes

Northwest Airlink Flight 5719: the worst aircraft disaster in Minnesota history killed 18

Large plane crashes in Minnesota have been mercifully rare; the largest passenger crash occurred outside Hibbing, Minnesota, in 1993. The plane, which clipped a tree due to pilot error, led to the deaths of 18 people.[1] Given that Minneapolis-St. Paul's airport is one of the busiest in the country, the lack of a major air disaster is impressive.[2]

Two famous crashes involving smaller planes

While large plane crashes have been uncommon in Minnesota, small plane crashes have taken their toll in Minnesota history. In 1959, a plane crash killed Buddy Holly, the Big Bopper and Ritchie Valens in what was later famously dubbed "Day the Music Died." (The trio's ultimate destination? A concert in Moorhead, Minnesota.) Minnesota also lost one of its political legends when U.S. Senator Paul Wellstone died in a tragic crash outside of Eveleth, Minnesota, in 2002, just days before a U.S. Senate election. Wellstone's wife, Sheila, and his daughter, Marcia, also died in the crash.

The I-35W Bridge Disaster

One of the busiest bridges in the Twin Cities fell 116 feet into the Mississippi[1]

One of the busiest bridges in Minneapolis, the I-35W bridge collapsed on August 1, 2007, during the height of rush hour. The final National Transportation Safety Board report indicated that the bridge collapsed because its initial design was flawed. The bridge's gusset plates, which support the trusses on the bridge, were not strong enough to support the expected load on the bridge, even under normal circumstances. The post-disaster investigation concluded that damage to the gusset plate that eventually failed had actually been detected prior to 1999; unfortunately, relatively little attention was given to gusset plates in inspections, as inspections usually looked for problems with the existing bridge structure, not flaws in the original bridge design.

A bad design and too much weight on the bridge sent 17 cars into the water

Unfortunately, on the day of the disaster, there was more weight on the bridge than usual. Construction work had shut down four of the eight lanes on the bridge, and heavy sand and gravel were positioned on the bridge deck. Previous bridge modifications had also made the bridge heavier, and at 6:05 p.m. on August 1, 2007, the bridge collapsed. The bridge broke into three parts. The center portion of the bridge fell straight downward into the river, and the north and south ends of the bridge each broke into smaller sections that were pitched at incredible angles. In all, 111 cars were on the section of the bridge that collapsed, including a school bus carrying 63 children, all of whom were rescued. Not everyone was so lucky; 17 cars were submerged in the Mississippi, and 13 people were killed.[2] The accident also injured 145, many seriously. If it weren't for impromptu rescue crews and first-responders, the toll would likely have been much higher.

The I-35W bridge disaster

Fires

The Hinckley Fire of 1894 killed 400 and burned 400 square miles

By the turn of the twentieth century, most of Minnesota's forests were gone. Clear-cutting didn't just lead to barren forests; it also left deadwood and debris everywhere, creating the perfect conditions for an uncontrolled wildfire. Just such a fire occurred on September 1, 1894, near Hinckley, Minnesota. A thriving city, small fires weren't unheard of nearby; usually set by passing trains, several were burning on that morning. But that morning was different: The area was undergoing what is called a "temperature inversion." Usually, the atmosphere gets colder as you get higher up. Sometimes, however, this relationship flips, creating a layer of cold air with a warmer layer above it. This layer can be thought of as a cap, and if that cap is breached, the layers will begin to equalize, with cold air rushing downward.[1] Under normal circumstances, this can lead to strong thunderstorms or tornadoes. Unfortunately for Hinckley, a brisk wind fanned the flames of the small fires burning around town. This "punctured" the inversion, causing cold air to rush down, feeding the fire and creating strong winds.[2] It's not much of an exaggeration to say that the result was a tornado made of fire.

Hinckley after the fire

Hinckley before the fire

The fire was so hot, the railroad tracks melted

The destruction was total—the fire was so hot that glass windows broke from the heat and the railroad tracks melted. People took cover wherever they could, in wells and rivers, but often to no avail. Many died of suffocation or were burned to death—this is even true for some people who were found in rivers. In the end, more than 400 people died (exact totals are unknown because some bodies simply were never found) and 400 square miles were burned. The fire was front-page news nationwide, and today the Hinckley Fire Museum remembers the carnage.

Many more would have been killed if not for a train that drove backwards

Many residents of Hinckley were saved due to the heroism and bravery of their friends and neighbors. One of the most famous stories of the Hinckley fire involves engineer James Root, who led his train into Hinckley only to find the town on fire. Desperate citizens rushed onto the train, and Root managed to drive it backwards, essentially racing the flames, for miles.[3] In the process, the train caught fire, the glass shattered from the heat, and Root was seriously injured, but they reached the relative safety of Skunk Lake, a shallow marsh that saved the passengers and crew from the flames.

The train engine that rescued so many

> **TRIVIA TIDBIT:** James Corbett, the Union soldier who shot John Wilkes Booth, probably died in the Hinckley fire.[4]

> **TALK ABOUT EERIE:** Another well-known figure in the Hinckley Fire was Tommy Dunn, the telegraph operator at the Hinckley Depot.[5] He heroically alerted nearby stations of the fire and summoned rescue crews. Dunn died in the fire; his last transmission read, "I think I've stayed too long."

Cloquet's fires killed 450 and burned over 1,000 square miles

The Hinckley Fire wasn't the only massive wildfire to strike Minnesota. In 1918, Cloquet was hit by a positively huge series of blazes that killed more than 450 people in a single day, burning a total of over 1,500 square miles.[6]

> **TRIVIA TIDBIT:** During World War II, the Japanese, well aware of the damage that fire could cause, attempted to set fire to the forests of the western U.S. by launching thousands of fire balloons. These balloons, which were launched into the jet stream, contained bombs that were intended to start fires and kill civilians. While the Japanese launched several thousand, only a few hundred were found, and only one killed any Americans, detonating after it was found by a minister's wife and five Sunday school children, killing all of them.[7,8]

> **TRIVIA TIDBIT:** The former fire chief of Babbitt, Minnesota, was recently arrested for setting several forest fires in Superior National Forest. He has been diagnosed with pyromania.

Mill and Industrial Disasters

A dangerous line of work

As an industrial hotspot, Minneapolis was not immune to industrial accidents, and the city's busy mills were filled with machines, belts and systems that could easily kill workers if the employees weren't careful. Workers were usually quite aware of such dangers, but an enormous disaster occurred on May 2, 1878, when highly inflammable flour dust in the huge Washburn "A" Mill exploded, killing 18 workers and destroying the entire facility and many buildings in the immediate vicinity. The disaster made national news and temporarily knocked out much of the flour-producing capacity in the state. The plant was rebuilt in relatively short order. Abandoned in the 1960s, it is now the site of the Mill City Museum.[1]

A vintage Washburn-Crosby ad, courtesy of the General Mills Archives

A vintage Washburn-Crosby ad, courtesy of the General Mills Archives

> **TRIVIA TIDBIT:** How dangerous was work in the mills? Well, let's put it this way: Minneapolis soon became known for pioneering in another field—the creation of artificial limbs.[2] Workers injured at the mills and at riverside factories often lost their limbs, and companies—including the Winkley Company, still in existence—sprang up to offer prosthetics.[3]

Other Disasters and Accidents of Note

If you try to "thaw out" dynamite over a fire, it'll probably explode

In 1897, a farmer living in Hermantown was planning to use some dynamite to get rid of stumps on his land. But he needed to "thaw it out" first and proceeded to do so by heating it . . . over a fire. Naturally, it exploded, destroying the whole house and killing the farmer. Tragically, two of his young sons were killed, and his wife and another son were seriously injured.

Santa Claus visited Grand Marais by airplane, crashed into the town movie theater

Maybe he should stick with the sleigh.[1] Around Christmas in 1949, Santa Claus was set to visit Grand Marais, Minnesota, and he was traveling by airplane. Unfortunately, after landing on the town's Main Street, the plane crashed headlong into the movie theater's marquee. Thankfully, Santa emerged unhurt, but there was no word on the fate of any presents aboard.

Crime

Dillinger's Colt pistol

FROM JOHN DILLINGER TO
THE GLENSHEEN MURDERS,
OUR STATE'S CRIMINAL
HISTORY MAKES IT CLEAR
THAT MINNESOTA ISN'T
ALWAYS "MINNESOTA NICE"

The Twin Cities have a long history of crime and corruption

For much of Minnesota's history, the Twin Cities were rightfully considered hotbeds of crime and corruption. Examples abound: in the 1880s, Minneapolis Mayor "Doc" Ames took bribes from just about everyone he could—petty offenders all the way up to major crime bosses.[1] He appointed his brother as police chief and then proceeded to fire police officers and replace them with crooks (who also would pay him bribes).[2] Eventually, Ames was removed from power, and the city's corruption became well-known, thanks to an exposé called *The Shame of Minneapolis*, which was published in *McClure's* and written by the journalist Lincoln Steffens.

"Doc" Ames

Jesse James, Cole Younger and the Northfield Raid

One of the most famous crimes in Minnesota history occurred on September 7, 1876, when a gang of eight robbers led by Jesse James and Cole Younger (commonly called the James-Younger gang) attempted to rob the First National Bank of Northfield, Minnesota. The robbery quickly went south, as Joseph Lee Haywood, the bank teller, refused to open the safe and even tried to lock one of the robbers in the vault. Haywood was soon pistol-whipped and gashed with a knife; outside, all hell was breaking loose, as the townsfolk had assembled with weapons and opened fire on the robbers, killing two gang members and wounding others. The robbers soon fled but not before killing Haywood; in the shootout, a bystander (Nicholas Gustafson) was also killed. The gang split up; the James brothers managed to avoid being caught, but the Younger brothers were apprehended relatively quickly and went to prison. Jesse James was eventually killed by one of his own men (who was out for a reward) and Frank James famously retired from crime, was tried (and acquitted) and lived a relatively normal life thereafter.

Jesse James

The Duluth lynchings of 1920

From the late 1880s through the 1960s, lynching was a pandemic in the U.S.; at least 5,000 people, most of them black, were lynched nationwide.[3] While commonly thought to be a crime that occurred in the South, lynchings weren't unheard of in Minnesota. At least nine lynchings occurred in the state; the most well-known are the Duluth lynchings of 1920.[4] The John Robinson Circus was in town in June of that year, and it employed a number of African-American workers. As the circus was packing up to leave, a white couple, Irene Tusken and James Sullivan, watched as the workers were tearing down the circus tents and preparing to transport them to the next town.[5] Soon thereafter, Sullivan reported that he had been held at knifepoint and Tusken had been raped. Later that evening, the police were informed, and the train, which was nearly ready to leave, was halted. Thirteen innocent African-American workers were taken off for questioning. Seven were released, and six were taken to the police station. By now, word had gotten out about the alleged attack, and despite the analysis of a local doctor (who determined that Tusken hadn't been raped), wild rumors began to spread. By the next evening a huge crowd had formed. This mob eventually broke into the police station and held an impromptu kangaroo trial, deeming Isaac McGhie, Elmer Jackson and Elias Clayton guilty.[6] The three were then dragged to a lamppost, where they were each lynched. After the murders, the mob lingered, taking souvenirs and photographs with the dead bodies, one of which was horrifyingly distributed as a postcard. Today, a memorial stands to honor the three murdered men.

St. Paul was a criminal safe haven during the early part of the twentieth century

Minneapolis wasn't the only place in Minnesota that was corrupt. From the turn of the century to the 1930s the city of St. Paul was known as a safe haven for criminals all over the country, thanks to what has been called "the O'Connor System," an unwritten agreement between police chief John O'Connor, the St. Paul Police Department and criminals.[7] In short, police turned a blind eye if criminals stayed in St. Paul, as long as

Part of John Dillinger's FBI file

```
WANTED      BANK ROBB.

JOHN DILLINGER, white,
lbs., 5'7½" tall, light
grey eyes, med. comp.
SCARS & MARKS: Cut cic. 5,
base of middle finger.
Any information or if loc
the Indiana State Police,
State House, Indianapolis,
nearest Sheriff or Police

P.P.C.  (13)
            9  R  O
           14  U  00
```

they committed no crimes while in the city and paid bribes to the police department. This system brought in just about every major criminal you could imagine—from John Dillinger and Baby Face Nelson to Machine Gun Kelly and the Barker-Karpis gang.[8] (Dillinger and his gang even got into a shootout with the FBI and the St. Paul Police; Dillinger managed to escape because the cops forgot to guard the back door.[9])

Machine Gun Kelly mugshot

> **TRIVIA TIDBIT:** Bonnie and Clyde also made their way into Minnesota, robbing a bank in Okabena in 1933.

Staying in St. Paul but robbing Minneapolis

Even though the O'Connor System ostensibly prevented criminals from committing crimes in St. Paul, there was no prohibition on committing crimes in nearby cities, including just across the river in Minneapolis. This policy led to an odd variety of self-enforcement in St. Paul; some criminals prevented others from committing crimes in St. Paul in order to maintain the status quo. Eventually, citizens mobilized to overturn the system.

Chief John O'Connor

Minnesota: site of one of the first car bombings

Toward the end of the O'Connor System, one of the more spectacular crimes in Minnesota history occurred: Minnesota saw its first car bombing and one of the first recorded in history. The bombing, which mortally injured Irish mob boss "Dapper" Danny Hogan, occurred in 1928 and was likely orchestrated by a rival who sought to take over Hogan's illicit businesses.[10]

The Hamm's Kidnapping: in the land of sky blue waters...there was a kidnapping

Two of the most high-profile crimes to occur in Minnesota were kidnappings. The first involved the kidnapping of Theo Hamm, the president of Hamm's Brewery. Hamm was kidnapped by Alvin "Creepy" Karpis and his gang, who demanded $100,000 in ransom. The ransom was delivered, and Hamm was released. However, the crooks were eventually tracked down, in part because of evidence they left behind—latent fingerprints that were discovered using a new fingerprinting technique (silver nitrate).[11]

Charles Lindbergh

The Lindbergh kidnapping

The first person to fly nonstop across the Atlantic, Charles Lindbergh was arguably the most famous person on the planet for a time. On March 1, 1932, his infant son was kidnapped from the family home; a broken homemade ladder was found outside the child's window. A ransom note demanding $50,000 soon arrived, beginning a convoluted process of additional ransom notes, shady go-betweens and attempts to secure the safety of the baby. Somewhat inexplicably, John Condon, a high school principal from New York, offered himself up as an intermediary with the kidnapper, even adding an extra $1,000 to the ransom. Lindbergh agreed and over the course of two months, Condon served as the primary person communicating with the kidnapper. It was like something out of a bad spy movie. Condon placed messages to the kidnapper via surreptitious newspaper ads, and the kidnapper responded in turn with messages that were delivered by cab drivers or by directing Condon to look for additional messages hidden in secret locations. Eventually Condon had a face-to-face meeting with "John" who claimed to be the kidnapper and gave Condon a piece of the child's clothing as proof. This back-and-forth process continued until Condon eventually delivered the money on April 2, and he was told the baby could be found on a boat in Martha's Vineyard. Unfortunately, the search turned up fruitless, and the baby's body was eventually discovered in May.[12] This didn't stop the investigation, however, and careful tracking of the serial numbers of the ransom money helped narrow down where it was being used and, eventually, by whom. In

1934, the home of Bruno Walter Hauptmann was raided, and a significant portion of the ransom bills was found in his garage.[13] A (largely circumstantial) case was built, and he was found guilty and executed. The rest of the money remains unaccounted for.

Glensheen Mansion and a crime straight out of *Clue*

If you're from Minnesota, you've probably heard of the Glensheen Mansion. A sprawling, 38-room mansion, the building is as famous for being a one-time crime scene as it is for its architecture. Elisabeth Congdon, the heiress to the mansion, was murdered here, along with her nurse, in the late 1970s. And as if the story was straight out of the board game *Clue*, the nurse was murdered in a corridor, with a candlestick. Sadly, that isn't a joke. The second husband of Elisabeth Congdon's adopted daughter, Marjorie, was the prime suspect and was later found guilty. Five years later, his conviction was overturned and he reached a plea deal with prosecutors in exchange for a confession to the murders and time served. He committed suicide in 1988.

Glensheen Mansion

The case of the missing slippers

Everyone knows Judy Garland from her role as Dorothy in *The Wizard of Oz*, but did you know she was born in Minnesota? She was born in Grand Rapids in 1922, although her birth name was Frances Ethel Gumm. She didn't become "Judy Garland" until 1935.

During the summer of 2005, a pair of Garland's famed red slippers from *The Wizard of Oz* (one of only four pairs in existence) was stolen from the Judy Garland Museum in Grand Rapids. The shoes are worth about $2 million and have not been recovered.

A Brief Look at Sports

FROM THE TWINS AND THE VIKINGS TO THE WILD AND THE T-WOLVES, WE MINNESOTANS TAKE OUR SPORTS SERIOUSLY. BECAUSE THE SUBJECT MATTER IS SO VAST, THIS IS SIMPLY A BRIEF INTRODUCTION TO THE "BIG FOUR" MINNESOTA SPORTS TEAMS

The Minnesota Twins (1961-Present)

FOUNDED IN MINNESOTA: 1961
PREVIOUS TEAM: The Washington Senators (officially known as the Nationals): 1901-1960[1]
WORLD SERIES APPEARANCES (BOTH TEAMS): 1924, 1925, 1933, 1965, 1987, 1991[2]
WORLD SERIES WINS (BOTH TEAMS): 1924, 1987, 1991

Twins Tidbits

Longest home runs by a Twin: Metropolitan Stadium: 520 feet, Harmon Killebrew; Metrodome: 480 feet, Kent Hrbek; Target Field: 490 feet, Jim Thome

Longest home run ever? A highly controversial question, analysis by a physicist and historical research by baseball author Jane Leavy indicates Mickey Mantle hit a home run on April 17, 1953, which traveled at least 535 feet.[3] (By the way, the fastest pitch recorded in MLB history was Aroldis Chapman's 105 mile-per-hour heater.)

Ticket inflation: When Metropolitan Stadium—the Twins' first home—opened, the most expensive ticket was $3. Today at Target Field, it's more than $120.[4]

Some familiar seasons: As all Twins fans know, the team has endured some rough seasons. In fact, Twins fans will probably relate to a famous quip about the Senators: First in war, first in peace, last in the American League.

The Minnesota Vikings (1961-Present)

FOUNDED IN MINNESOTA: 1961[5]
SUPER BOWL APPEARANCES: 1969, 1973, 1974, 1976
SUPER BOWL WINS: You already know the answer.

Vikings Tidbits

The Most Points Scored? Purple and Gold: Two former Vikings are tops when it comes to total points scored in league history. Morten Andersen scored 2,544 points, and Gary Anderson scored 2,434 points. (If Anderson had made the kick we all remember, it would have been 2,437.) Jerry Rice is the highest-rated non-kicker, with 1,256 points.[6]

The infamous trade: In 1989 running back Herschel Walker was traded from the Dallas Cowboys to the Minnesota Vikings for a whopping 11 players in all (including five draft picks that would net the Cowboys Emmitt Smith and Darren Woodson, among others). Under incredible pressure in Minnesota, Walker didn't perform as anticipated, and the trade became one of the most reviled in team history. Walker's story didn't end there. He competed in the Olympics as a bobsledder, has championed mental health awareness (diagnosed with dissociative identity disorder, Walker doesn't remember any of his Heisman-winning season) and has since recorded two victories in mixed martial arts—at the age of 48.

Alan Page: One of the finest players in team history, defensive tackle Alan Page is a member of the NFL Hall of Fame, yet while he was racking up tackles and recovering fumbles, he was also working on his law degree. You read that right: He was playing pro football and getting his Juris Doctor on the side. Once his career ended, he entered another venerated hall: the Minnesota Supreme Court—where he has been an associate justice since 1993.[7]

The Minnesota Timberwolves (1989-Present)

FOUNDED IN MINNESOTA: 1989
PREVIOUS TEAM IN MINNESOTA: The Minneapolis Lakers (1947-1960)
NBA FINALS APPEARANCES: 6 (as the Lakers)
NBA TITLES: 1949, 1950, 1952, 1953, 1954, 1959[8]

T-Wolves Tidbits

The First Dynasty: Like the L.A. Lakers of recent memory, in the late 1940s and early 1950s, the Minneapolis Lakers were the first NBA dynasty, winning five championships. Their general manager? None other than Sid Hartman, the *StarTribune* columnist. The finest player on

the Lakers? George Mikan, the 6'10" center whose tough play revolutionized basketball, leading to the big men of today.

Kevin Love and a Famous Band: Without question, Kevin Love is one of the finest players to wear a Timberwolves jersey; oddly enough, he's also related to Mike Love, one of the founding members of the Beach Boys. Mike is Kevin's uncle.[9]

Kevin Garnett and Soccer: An ardent soccer fan, Timberwolves great Kevin Garnett owns a small stake in A.C. Roma, a team in Italy's top soccer league.

The Minnesota Wild (1997-Present)

FOUNDED IN MINNESOTA: 1997
PREVIOUS TEAM IN MINNESOTA: The Minnesota North Stars (1967-1993)
STANLEY CUP APPEARANCES: 1981, 1991 (as the North Stars)[10]
STANLEY CUP WINS: None

Wild Tidbits

What's in a Name? Once Minnesota was granted a new NHL team, one of the first problems was determining a name. There were six options in all: the Blue Ox, the Freeze, the Northern Lights, the Voyageurs, the White Bears and the Wild, which eventually won out.[11]

A Familiar Palette: The Wild's official colors are forest green, Iron Range red, harvest gold, Minnesota wheat, and white.

The Odd Destinations of Our Teams: When the North Stars left for Dallas, Texas, it wasn't the first time a Minnesota team moved to a city where its name didn't make any sense. After all, the "North" Stars moved to Texas, a state that shares the same latitude as portions of the Sahara. Decades before, the Minneapolis Lakers went from the Land of 10,000 Lakes to Los Angeles, a city where many of the lakes are man-made and where the Los Angeles River was essentially replaced with a series of concrete channels.

Quirky Minnesota

WITH GIANT ROADSIDE SCULPTURES, STRANGE LAWS AND SOME ODD MUSEUMS, MINNESOTA HAS ENOUGH ROADSIDE ATTRACTIONS AND ODDITIES TO INTEREST ALMOST ANYONE

"Crazy" Laws and Reality

Almost all of the absurd laws attributed to Minnesota aren't real. Perhaps the most famous is the notion that it's illegal to walk across the state border with a duck on your head. (Never mind the fact that such an act would be a federal crime, a violation of the Migratory Bird Act.)

Some alleged "stupid laws" refer to long-defunct laws in other states, whereas others are simply made up. That doesn't mean that Minnesota law doesn't have its quirks, however. In fact, if you look through the Minnesota Statutes, there's plenty of interesting and strange information buried in the legalese.

That venerable tradition: an open season on frogs

Believe it or not, there is an open season for frogs in Minnesota. It lasts from May 16 to March 31, but only if the frogs are intended to be used as bait.[1]

Minnesota law bans "trafficking in skunks"

Somewhat amazingly, there is a heading in the Minnesota Statutes that reads "TRAFFICKING IN SKUNKS."[2] (It bans the import of skunks given the very-real fear of rabies, but it's hard not to imagine a cartoonish, if bizarre, crime syndicate of some sort.)

A few legal misconceptions, and illegal activities that might surprise you

It's illegal for morticians to assert that dead bodies must be embalmed.[3] (It's only required under specific circumstances.)

Hitchhiking is illegal in Minnesota, and so is panhandling.[4]

Technically, adultery is still a crime in Minnesota. It is punishable by up to a year in jail and a fine of $3,000.[5] Fornication is still on the books, too.[6]

It's illegal for an employer (prospective or otherwise) to compel you to take a lie detector test.[7]

It is legal to breastfeed in public. Minnesota law specifically exempts breastfeeding moms from indecent exposure laws.[8]

If you are forced into a settlement with a court and your wages are garnished and your property seized, the court can't take every-thing.[9] Within certain limits, you can retain a car, farming equipment (if you're a farmer) and perhaps more oddly, the state cannot also seize "The family Bible, library, or musical instruments." Individuals also get to retain "all wearing apparel and one watch," among other things.

Pay toilets are illegal in public buildings and places in Minnesota.[10]

Because of the Migratory Bird Treaty, it's illegal to collect feathers, nests or eggs of most common bird species. The treaty covers most familiar popular species. Game species are often fair game (ha?), however. The Treaty was originally enacted after feather collection (often for hats) led to the near-extinction of many bird species, including the Great Egret, which was hunted for its beautiful aigrettes.

Great Egret

According to Minnesota law, "a person does not need a turtle seller's license or an angling license" if they plan "to take, possess, and rent or sell up to 25 turtles greater than four inches in length for the purpose of providing the turtles to participants at a nonprofit turtle race."[11] Longville, Minnesota, the proclaimed "turtle capital of the world" is particularly well-known for its turtle races.

According to state law, you can be charged with Rioting in the Third Degree (or the second or the first).[12]

The Church Lady Law

Minnesota, famous for its church suppers, has a law that mandates food safety training for those overseeing church luncheons, potlucks and the like. (It was popularly dubbed the Hot Dish Law or the Church Lady Law and passed after some serious health issues arose at church suppers due to food safety violations.)

What's your defense against wolves? Mine: a donkey

In the northern part of the state, where wolf populations are rebounding, wolf predation of livestock (and pets!) is a concern. In addition to compensation in the event of a confirmed wolf kill, Minnesota allows residents to post guard animals. That's where things get a little weird. According to Minnesota Statute, the term "guard animal" refers to (and I'm quoting) "a donkey, llama, dog, or other domestic animal specifically bred, trained, and used to protect livestock, domestic animals, or pets."[13] So if wolf predation is a problem in your area, rest assured: you can always hire a donkey mercenary.

Strange Minnesota

St. Urho, the (invented) Finnish Response to St. Patrick

St. Urho

Perhaps tired of the prominence of St. Patrick's Day, Minnesota's Finnish population now celebrates St. Urho's Day, which just so happens to occur the day before everyone dons green and pretends to be Irish.[14] The holiday was invented in the 1950s and has since been heartily embraced by the Finnish population of Minnesota and even in Finland. As for the saint himself, St. Urho was reputed to have driven all of the frogs or grasshoppers (it depends on the telling) from Finland, thereby saving the grape harvest. (Given that grapes don't grow well in Finland, that should be enough to tell you the story is legend.)

Minnesota, land of 10,000 zombies?

For a brief time, Minneapolis held the Guinness World Record for the largest recorded gathering of zombies.[15] The Minneapolis Zombie Pub Crawl originally held the record, with over 8,000 zombie-clad participants in attendance, but nearly 10,000 members of New Jersey's undead have since claimed the record.

Minneapolis and St. Paul once disagreed about Daylight Savings Time and set their clocks one hour apart

For a few weeks in 1965, the cities of Minneapolis and St. Paul couldn't agree on what time it was. St. Paul wanted its clock to align with the rest of the country, but Minneapolis wanted to adhere to state law. They couldn't come to an agreement, so for a few weeks, the two cities were an hour apart.[16] As similar problems played out nationwide, Congress soon passed a law specifying a uniform Daylight Savings Time.

Underwater logging was briefly legal in Minnesota

During the heyday of Minnesota logging, millions of logs were floated down Minnesota lakes and rivers. Not all of them made it, and some survive today as "deadheads" or logs that are found at the bottom of Minnesota lakes. Somewhat amazingly, the State of Minnesota once allowed these logs to be logged underwater, as they are property of the state.[17] Would-be "underwater loggers" needed a permit, however.

The Stone Arch Bridge

The famed Stone Arch Bridge was originally dubbed a mistake

Built by railroad tycoon James J. Hill, Minneapolis' Stone Arch Bridge was originally considered a mistake and named "Hill's Folly" because of its expense.[8] It has since become one of the defining landmarks of the Twin Cities.

A tongue-in-cheek rebuttal of a disaster

Minnesota State University Moorhead's athletic teams were originally known as the "Fighting Pedagogues" (pedagogy has to do with the art and science of teaching). The main building of the school, then known as Moorhead Teachers College, burned down. The school rebuilt, and the team name was changed. The school's new name? The Dragons.

Climax city hall

Let's talk about Climax and Embarrass, Minnesota

Some Minnesota cities and towns have strange names—the city of Climax in Polk County is a good example. Thankfully, Embarrass, Minnesota, is quite some distance away, as it is in St. Louis County. If the two towns were neighbors, one could only imagine the colorful cheers one might hear at a sporting event. Oddly, Climax was actually named after a tobacco company. Embarrass was named for the nearby Embarrass River, which was quite difficult to navigate.

Climax was in the national news a few years ago due to a controversy over the town's centennial.[19] The slogan "More than a feeling" was selected after a contest was held in 1996 to determine the motto. Other contenders were reportedly, "No End to Climax," "Cling to the Culmination: Climax Forever" and "Bring a Friend to Climax."

This led to a bit of national controversy: High school students wearing shirts bearing the town's slogan at the local Climax-Shelly High School were sent home by school officials who deemed the slogan inappropriate.

Want to see a giant sunfish? A real glockenspiel? How about Pierre, the pantsless voyageur? Minnesota is the place

Yes, all of those things really exist in Minnesota, which is as famous for its strange statuary and odd attractions as it is for its walleye and hot dish. This is just a sampling of the odd statues, monuments and activities you can find in the state. For Paul Bunyan statues, see page 12.

ALEXANDRIA: Big Ole, a statue of a viking

BENA: A restaurant inside a building shaped like a large northern pike

BLUE EARTH: Jolly Green Giant statue

CUYUNA: Wood tick races

DARWIN: Largest ball of twine

DEERWOOD: Giant deer statue

EVELETH: Largest free-standing hockey stick[20]

FERGUS FALLS: World's largest otter

GARRISON: Giant walleye statue

The world's largest ball of twine in Darwin

INTERNATIONAL FALLS: Smokey Bear statue[21]

KABETOGAMA: Giant walleye statue you can sit on

LONGVILLE: Turtle races

MORA: Giant dala horse (an iconic Swedish knickknack)

MOORHEAD: Re-created Viking ship

NEW ULM: Statue of Herman the German (the leader of an ancient Germanic tribe that walloped the Romans); New Ulm also boasts a real Glockenspiel

OLIVIA: World's largest ear of corn

ORR: Giant sunfish

OUTING: Frog races

PELICAN RAPIDS: A giant pelican

SILVER BAY: Rocky Taconite, a mascot for the nearby iron-mining industry

ROTHSAY: Giant prairie chicken

NORTH ST. PAUL: Giant stucco snowman[22]

TWO HARBORS: Pierre, the Voyageur (he's really not wearing pants; it's darn odd)

VIRGINIA: World's largest floating loon[23]

WALKER: The Eelpout Festival

The giant prairie chicken in Rothsay

A Sampling of Minnesota's Museums

Art museums

From the Minneapolis Institute of Arts (http://new.artsmia.org) and the Walker Art Museum (www.walkerart.org) to the University of Minnesota's Weisman Museum (www.weisman.umn.edu) and Winona's Maritime Art Museum (www.mmam.org), Minnesota is home to a wide variety of art museums. Whatever your taste in art, you're sure to find it in Minnesota.

Bakken Museum (www.thebakken.org)

The Bakken Museum is literally electric. Dedicated to the science and history of electricity, the Minneapolis museum is chock full of exhibits, hands-on activities and more.

Bell Museum of Natural History (www.bellmuseum.umn.edu)

Located on the campus of the University of Minnesota, the Bell Museum is home to one of the finest natural history collections in Minnesota.

Dorothy Molter Museum (www.rootbeerlady.com)

Dorothy Molter was known as the "Root Beer Lady" and lived alone in the Boundary Waters Canoe Area Wilderness for decades. She was famous for selling her handmade root beer to thirsty canoeists and visitors, and she holds an important place in Minnesota history.

Great Lakes Floating Maritime Museum (http://www.decc.org/william-a-irvin)

Dedicated to the maritime history of Minnesota and the Great Lakes, this Duluth museum is home to several vessels, including the 610-foot ore freighter, *William A. Irvin*. The ships can be toured and are home to many events.

Hinckley Fire Museum (http://hinckleyfiremuseum.com)

The infamous Hinckley Fire of 1894 absolutely leveled Hinckley and much of the surrounding area, and Hinckley's Fire Museum commemorates the heroism of those who helped rescue victims from the fire and the lives of the fire's many victims.

Lower Sioux Agency Interpretive Center (http://sites.mnhs.org/historic-sites/lower-sioux-agency)

Memorializing the history of the 1862 U.S.-Dakota War, the Lower Sioux Agency was ground zero for the beginnings of the conflict. Located in Morton, the site offers a history center, exhibits, original structures and tours.

Mille Lacs Indian Museum and Trading Post (http://sites.mnhs.org/historic-sites/mille-lacs-indian-museum)

Dedicated to the history and culture of the Ojibwe people in Minnesota, this Onamia museum features exhibits, events, activities and artwork for sale made by American Indians.

Minnesota History Center (www.minnesotahistorycenter.org)

Run by the Minnesota Historical Society, St. Paul's Minnesota History Center is the go-to source for information about Minnesota's history and features exhibits, artifacts and public records.

Science Museum of Minnesota (www.smm.org)

With a commanding view of the Mississippi River in St. Paul, the Science Museum of Minnesota boasts special exhibits, dinosaur fossils, an Omnimax Theater, dozens of interactive exhibits and a variety of activities for children and adults.

SPAM Museum (www.spam.com/spam-101/the-spam-museum)

A museum chronicling the history of Hormel's most famous product, SPAM, this Austin museum includes exhibits about SPAM in World War II, SPAM and Monty Python, and more.

The Works (http://www.theworks.org)

With dozens of fun, hands-on activities, Bloomington's Works Museum is a great way to introduce your children (or yourself!) to the wonders of science and engineering.

Bibliography

A Glance at Minnesota (and Minnesotans)

1. "Minnesota QuickFacts from the U.S. Census Bureau." Minnesota QuickFacts from the U.S. Census Bureau. http://quickfacts.census.gov/qfd/states/27000.html

2. "Grand Portage State Park." Minnesota Department of Natural Resources. http://www.dnr.state.mn.us/state_parks/grand_portage/index.html

3. "United States Census Bureau." Incorporated Places and Minor Civil Divisions Datasets: Subcounty Resident Population Estimates: April 1, 2010 to July 1, 2012. http://www.census.gov/popest/data/cities/totals/2012/SUB-EST2012.html

4. "Minnesota State Demographic Center." State Demographic Center. http://www.demography.state.mn.us/Census2010/

5. Brower, Susan. "Cargill Retirees (PowerPoint)." http://www.demography.state.mn.us/documents/SusanBrower_Cargill_Jan2014.pdf

6. "Minnesota QuickFacts from the U.S. Census Bureau." Minnesota QuickFacts from the U.S. Census Bureau. http://quickfacts.census.gov/qfd/states/27000.html

7. American Veterinary Medical Association. "U.S. Pet Ownership & Demographics Sourcebook (2012)." U.S. Pet Ownership & Demographics Sourcebook (2012). https://www.avma.org/KB/Resources/Statistics/Pages/Market-research-statistics-US-Pet-Ownership-Demographics-Sourcebook.aspx.

8. IMDB.com. "Biography: Andre the Giant." IMDB. http://www.imdb.com/name/nm0000764/bio

9. Muscleandfitness.com. "Arnold Confirms Andre the Giant's Legendary Generosity." Muscle & Fitness. http://www.muscleandfitness.com/news-and-features/athletes-and-celebrities/arnold-confirms-andre-giants-legendary-generosity

10. Schapiro, Rick. "Walter Breuning, world's oldest man, dies at age 114 in Montana." NY Daily News. http://www.nydailynews.com/news/national/walter-breuning-world-oldest-man-dies-age-114-montana-article-1.112562

11. MyFoxTwinCities.com. "5 Minnesotans make Forbes 400 Richest Americans list." KMSP-TV. http://www.myfoxtwincities.com/story/23441151/5-minnesotans-make-forbes-list-of-richest-americans

12. Minnesota Department of Administration. "DatasetPopulation density." Resource record: Population density. http://www.demography.state.mn.us/resource.html?Id=5238

13. U.S. Census Bureau. "New York County (Manhattan Borough) QuickFacts from the U.S. Census Bureau." New York County (Manhattan Borough) QuickFacts from the U.S. Census Bureau. http://quickfacts.census.gov/qfd/states/36/36061.html

14. Nosowitz, Dan. "Life Inside The Most Densely Populated Place On Earth [Infographic]." Popular Science. http://www.popsci.com/technology/article/2013-04/life-inside-most-densely-populated-place-earth-infographic

Paul Bunyan, Hot Dish and Other Minnesota Standards

1. VisitBemidji.com. "Paul Bunyan." Bemidji Minnesota Family Vacation. http://www.visitbemidji.com/bemidji/paulbabe.html

2. *Ibid.*

3. University of Wisconsin, Milwaukee. "Dialect Survey Results: Minnesota." Dialect Survey Results: Minnesota. http://www4.uwm.edu/FLL/linguistics/dialect/staticmaps/state_MN.html

4. Berczeller, Paul. "Death in the snow." The Guardian. http://www.theguardian.com/culture/2003/jun/06/artsfeatures1

5. Shortridge, Barbara. "Not Just Jello and Hot Dishes: Representative Foods of Minnesota." *Journal of Cultural Geography*. Fall/Winter 2003. 21:1(71-94). http://www.d.umn.edu/~lknopp/geog3702-90/Minnesota Food.pdf

6. MyFoxTwinCities.com. "10 hot dish recipes from Minnesota's congressional delegation." KMSP-TV. http://www.myfoxtwincities.com/story/24960566/hotdish-off-frozen-dessert-hotdish-ties-for-2nd-place.

7. Nordicware.com. "Heritage | Nordic Ware." Heritage | Nordic Ware. https://www.nordicware.com/our-story/heritage/#.Uz2P1BYSPIo

8. Hormel Foods. "Why is SPAM® Brand a Household Name?." SPAM. http://www.spam.com/spam-101/why-is-spam-a-household-brand

9. *Ibid.*

10. Janick, Erica. "Scandinavians' Strange Holiday Lutefisk Tradition." *Smithsonian*. http://www.smithsonianmag.com/people-places/scandinavians-strange-holiday-lutefisk-tradition-2218218/?no-ist

11. Kuhlmann, Charles B. "The Influence of the Minneapolis Flour Mills Upon the Economic Development of Minnesota and the Northwest." *Minnesota History Magazine*. http://collections.mnhs.org/MNHistoryMagazine/articles/6/v06i02p141-154.pdf

12. Danbom, David. "Flour Power: The Significance of Flour Milling at the Falls." *Minnesota History Magazine*. http://collections.mnhs.org/MNHistoryMagazine/articles/58/v58i05-06p270-285.pdf

13. U.S. Government Printing Office. "Weights and Measures for Flour-mill and Corn-mill Products, Etc.: Hearings Before the Committee on Coinage, Weights, and Measures, Sixty-seventh Congress, First Session, on H.R. 4901, a Bill to Establish the Standard of Weights and Measures for the Following Wheat-mill and Corn Products, Namely, Flours, Hominy Grits, and Meals, and All Commercial Feeding Stuffs, and for Other Purposes., Volume 66, Part 1. 1921."

14. Pennefeather, Shannon. *Mill City: A Visual History Of The Minneapolis Mill District*. Minnesota Historical Society Press. 2003.

15. Hornley, Stew. "St. Paul Unions, Minnesota's First Major League Team." St. Paul Unions. http://stewthornley.net/unions.html

16. Minnesota.cbslocal.com. "History of WCCO Radio - CBS Minnesota." CBS Minnesota. http://minnesota.cbslocal.com/2010/10/22/history-of-wcco-radio/ (accessed June 2, 2014)

Geology and Climate

1. University of Minnesota, Minnesota Geological Survey. "Minnesota at a Glance: Precambrian Geology." ftp://mgssun6.mngs.umn.edu/pub2/mnglance/Mn_Precambrian.pdf

2. Ojakangas, Richard W., and Charles L. Matsch. *Minnesota's Geology*. Minneapolis: University of Minnesota Press, 1982.

3. Jarzen, David M. "Eusporangiate Ferns from the Dakota Formation, Minnesota, U.S.A." *International Journal of Plant Sciences* 167: 579-589.

4. Lynch, Bob, and Dan R. Lynch. *Lake Superior Rocks & Minerals: A Field Guide to the Lake Superior Area*. Cambridge, MN: Adventure Publications, 2008.

5. Lynch, Dan R., and Bob Lynch. *Agates of Lake Superior: Stunning Varieties and How They Are Formed*. Cambridge, MN: Adventure Publications, 2011.

6. Moose Lake Chamber of Commerce. "Agate Days and Art in the Park." Moose Lake Area Chamber of Commerce. http://www.mooselakechamber.com/agate-days-and-art-in-the-park.php

7. The Cathedral of Valencia. "The History of the Holy Chalice." Catedral de Valencia ~ La Catedral del Santo Cáliz. http://www.catedraldevalencia.es/

8. Dietrich, R. V. "Thomsonite." GemRocks: Thomsonite. http://www.cst.cmich.edu/users/dietr1rv/thomsonite.htm

9. *Ibid.*

10. "Niagara Cave." Home. http://www.niagaracave.com/

11. "Wabasha Street Caves." Wabasha Street Caves. http://www.wabashastreetcaves.com

12. Minnesota Department of Natural Resources. "Minnesota Mining History." - Digging into MN Minerals: Minnesota DNR. http://www.dnr.state.mn.us/education/geology/digging/history.html

13. Polymet Mining. "Northmet Project Overview." http://www.polymetmining.com/northmet-project/overview/

14. Minnesota Department of Natural Resources. "Biomes of Minnesota: Minnesota DNR." http://dnr.state.mn.us/biomes/index.html

15. Minnesota Department of Natural Resources. "Prairie Grasslands" http://www.dnr.state.mn.us/snas/prairie_description.html

16. Frazier, Ian. "John Deere Was a Real Person, His Invention Changed the Country." *Smithsonian*. http://www.smithsonianmag.com/history/john-deere-was-a-real-person-his-invention-changed-the-country-4017033/?no-ist

17. Gibbon, Guy E. *Archaeology of Minnesota: the prehistory of the upper Mississippi river region*. Minneapolis: University of Minnesota Press, 2012.

18. *Ibid.*

19. *Ibid.*

20. *Ibid.*

21. *Ibid.*

22. Samenow, Jason. "New USDA plant zones clearly show climate change." Washington Post. http://www.washingtonpost.com/blogs/capital-weather-gang/post/new-usda-plant-zones-clearly-show-climate-change/2012/01/27/gIQA7Vz2VQ_blog.html

23. The Arbor Day Foundation. "Hardiness Zone Changes Between 1990 and 2006." The Arbor Day Foundation. https://www.arborday.org/media/map_change.cfm

Weather, Winter and Natural Disasters

1. National Climactic Data Center. "State Climate Extremes Committee (SCEC)." National Climatic Data Center (NCDC). http://www.ncdc.noaa.gov/extremes/scec/records

2. Minnesota Climatology Working Group. "Extreme 24 Hour Temperature Changes - January 29, 2008." Extreme 24 Hour Temperature Changes: January 29, 2008. http://climate.umn.edu/doc/journal/temperature_change080129.htm

3. National Weather Service Central Region Headquarters. "Minneapolis/St Paul Snowfall History." http://www.crh.noaa.gov/mpx/?n=mspsnowfall

4. Minnesota Department of Natural Resources. "Historical Chances of a White Christmas." http://www.dnr.state.mn.us/climate/summaries_and_publications/white_christmas.html

5. *Ibid.*

6. National Weather Service Central Region Headquarters. "Coldest Meteorological Winters - How Did This Winter Rank?" NWS Central Region Headquarters. http://www.crh.noaa.gov/

7. *USA Today*, "Minn. city wins trademark for 'Icebox' of the Nation." February 11, 2008.

8. National Weather Service Central Region Headquarters. "Minneapolis/St Paul Snowfall History." http://www.crh.noaa.gov/mpx/?n=mspsnowfall

9. Minnesota Climatology Working Group. "Daily Weather Records for the Twin Cities: 1910s." http://climate.umn.edu/doc/twin_cities/msp1910's.htm

10. Minnesota Climatology Working Group. "Extended Period of Zero or Below in the Twin Cities 1873-2014." http://climate.umn.edu/doc/journal/below_zero_streaks.htm

11. Minnesota Climatology Working Group. "Daily Weather Records for the Twin Cities: 1870s." http://climate.umn.edu/doc/twin_cities/msp1870's.htm

12. Minnesota Climatology Working Group. "Precipitation and Temperature Summary for January 2014." http://climate.umn.edu/cawap/monsum/1401.txt

13. Minnesota Department of Natural Resources. "Normals, Means and Extremes for International Falls, MN." http://files.dnr.state.mn.us/natural_resources/climate/summaries_and_publications/2005_Annual_LCD_INL_page_3.pdf

14. Seeley, Mark W. *Minnesota Weather Almanac*. St. Paul: Minnesota Historical Society Press, 2006.

15. Minnesota Climatology Working Group. "Minnesota's Historical Lake Ice-Out Dates." Minnesota's Historical Lake Ice-Out Dates. http://climate.umn.edu/doc/ice_out/ice_out_historical.htm

16. Minnesota Department of Natural Resources. "Fishing in Minnesota: Minnesota DNR." http://www.dnr.state.mn.us/fishing/index.html

17. *Minneapolis Tribune*. "Frogs Rain Down in Northeast Minneapolis." July 20, 1901.

Blizzards

1. St. Martin, Thomas. "With a bang, not a whimper: The Winter of 1887-1888." http://files.dnr.state.mn.us/natural_resources/climate/summaries_and_publications/mn_winter_1887-1888_revised.pdf

2. Ford, Alyssa. "125 years ago, deadly 'Children's Blizzard' blasted Minnesota." MinnPost. http://www.minnpost.com/minnesota-history/2013/01/125-years-ago-deadly-children-s-blizzard-blasted-minnesota

3. Minnesota Climatology Working Group. "Daily Weather Records for the Twin Cities: 1940s." http://climate.umn.edu/doc/twin_cities/msp1940's.htm

4. Minnesota Climatology Working Group. "Worst Weather Disasters, #2 1940 Armistice Day Blizzard." http://climate.umn.edu/doc/journal/top5/numbertwo.htm

5. Minnesota Public Radio. "The Winds of Hell." http://www.mprnews.org/story/200011/10_steilm_blizzard-m

6. Minnesota Department of Natural Resources. "Famous Winter Storms." http://www.dnr.state.mn.us/climate/summaries_and_publications/winter_storms.html

7. National Weather Service Weather Forecast Office. "Biggest Snowstorms In The United States From 1888 to Present." http://www.crh.noaa.gov/mkx/?n=biggestsnowstorms-us

8. Seeley, Mark W. *Minnesota weather almanac*. St. Paul: Minnesota Historical Society Press, 2006.

9. Blindauer KM, Rubin C, Morse DL, McGeehin M. "The 1996 New York blizzard: impact on noninjury emergency visits." *American Journal of Emergency Medicine*, 1999 Jan;17(1):23-7.

10. National Weather Service Weather Forecast Office. "The Halloween Blizzard of 1991." http://www.crh.noaa.gov/dlh/?n=1991halloweenblizzard

11. Weather.com. "Historic Halloween Storms: Perfect Storm, Blizzard of 1991 Top the List." http://www.weather.com/family-kids/holidays-halloween/historic-halloween-storms-20120910?pageno=3

12. Mcauliffe, Bill. "Halloween blizzard of '91 'A heck of a trick'." *StarTribune*, October 31, 2011. http://www.startribune.com/lifestyle/132858378.html

Droughts and Dust Storms

1. Monthly Weather Review. "Dust Storms, November 1933 to May 1934." http://docs.lib.noaa.gov/rescue/mwr/063/mwr-063-02-0053.pdf

2. Worster, Donald. "Dust Bowl," *Handbook of Texas Online*. http://www.tshaonline.org/handbook/online/articles/ydd01. Published by the Texas State Historical Association.

3. St. Martin, Tom. "Decade of Disconsolation." http://files.dnr.state.mn.us/natural_resources/climate/summaries_and_publications/decade_of_disconsolation.pdf

4. "Dust Pneumonia Blues." History Engine: Tools for Collaborative Education and Research | Episodes. http://historyengine.richmond.edu/episodes/view/5362

5. Kalis, Martin A. "Public Health and Drought." *Journal of Environmental Health.* July/August 2009. http://www.cdc.gov/nceh/ehs/Docs/JEH/2009/July-Aug_09_Kalis_Miller.pdf

6. Minnesota Department of Natural Resources. "The Drought of 1988." http://files.dnr.state.mn.us/natural_resources/climate/summaries_and_publications/drought1988.pdf

7. Minnesota Climatology Working Group. "Daily Weather Records for the Twin Cities: 1980s." http://climate.umn.edu/doc/twin_cities/msp1980's.htm

Tornadoes

1. Climate Data Online, NOAA. "Climate of Minnesota (Introduction)." http://cdo.ncdc.noaa.gov/climatenormals/clim60/states/Clim_MN_01.pdf

2. Minnesota Department of Natural Resources. "Minnesota Tornado History and Statistics." http://www.dnr.state.mn.us/climate/summaries_and_publications/tornadoes.html

3. U.S. Army Signal Corps. "Monthly Weather Review for April 1886." http://docs.lib.noaa.gov/rescue/mwr/014/mwr-014-04-0100b.pdf

4. The City of Sauk Rapids. "History." http://www.ci.sauk-rapids.mn.us/index.asp?Type=B_
BASIC&SEC=%7BBC290869-DC15-48C6-AABC-5B38E05EC174%7D

5. National Weather Service Weather Forecast Office. "The May 6, 1965 Tornadoes" Summary of May 6,
1965 Tornado Outbreak. http://www.crh.noaa.gov/mpx/HistoricalEvents/1965May06/

6. *Ibid.*

7. Minnesota Department of Natural Resources. "Minneapolis Tornado: May 22, 2011." http://www.dnr.
state.mn.us/climate/journal/tornado_110523.html

8. Minnesota Public Radio. "North Minneapolis tornado: One year later." http://minnesota.publicradio.org/
projects/2012/05/north-minneapolis-tornado-anniversary/

9. Keen, Judy. "North Minneapolis still struggling to recover from 2011 tornado." MinnPost http://www.
minnpost.com/cityscape/2013/10/north-minneapolis-still-struggling-recover-2011-tornado

10. Minnesota Department of Natural Resources. "Minnesota Tornado History and Statistics." http://www.
dnr.state.mn.us/climate/summaries_and_publications/tornadoes.html

Floods and Other Storms

1. The State of North Dakota. "North Dakota Response to the 1997 Disasters." http://www.nd.gov/des/
uploads%5Cresources%5C736%5Cn.d.-response-to-the-1997-disasters.pdf (accessed June 2, 2014)

2. National Weather Service Climate Prediction Service. "Red River Flood." Red River Flooding. http://www.
cpc.ncep.noaa.gov/products/assessments/assess_97/rriver.html

3. Minnesota Climatology Working Group. "25th Anniversary of the 1987 Twin Cities Superstorm: July
23-24, 1987." http://climate.umn.edu/doc/journal/870723_24_superstorm.htm

4. Kare11.com. "The July 23, 1987 Superstorm!" http://host-34.242.54.159.gannett.com/news/arti-
cle/519770/80/The-July-23-1987-Superstorm

5. Bureau of Labor Statistics. "CPI Inflation Calculator." CPI Inflation Calculator. http://data.bls.gov/cgi-bin/
cpicalc.pl

6. Storm Prediction Center (NOAA). "The Boundary Waters-Canadian Derecho." http://www.spc.noaa.gov/
misc/AbtDerechos/casepages/jul4-51999page.htm

Earthquakes

1. United States Geological Service. "Historic Earthquakes, Western Minnesota." http://earthquake.usgs.
gov/earthquakes/states/events/1975_07_09.php

Wildlife

1. Cornell Lab of Ornithology. "Common Loon." Life History, All About Birds. http://www.allaboutbirds.org/guide/common_loon/lifehistory

2. *Ibid.*

3. Grier, J. "Ban Of DDT And Subsequent Recovery Of Reproduction In Bald Eagles." *Science.* December 17, 1982. 1232-1235.

4. Minnesota Department of Natural Resources. "Animals native to Minnesota." http://www.dnr.state.mn.us/faq/mnfacts/animals.html

5. *Ibid.*

6. NBC News. "Teen survives first known wolf attack in Minnesota - NBC News." http://www.nbcnews.com/news/other/teen-survives-first-known-wolf-attack-minnesota-f8C11024436

7. Minneapolis StarTribune. "Deformed wolf that bit Minnesota teen had brain damage." http://www.startribune.com/local/225392642.html

8. Minnesota Department of Natural Resources. "Avoid deer-vehicle crashes while driving this fall: News Releases: Minnesota DNR." http://news.dnr.state.mn.us/2013/10/07/avoid-deer-vehicle-crashes-while-driving-this-fall/

9. U.S. Department of Transportation, Federal Highway Administration. "Wildlife-Vehicle Collision Reduction Study: Report To Congress." Chapter 2. http://www.fhwa.dot.gov/publications/research/safety/08034/02.cfm#sec05

10. Deer Vehicle Crash Information Clearinghouse. "National Animal-Vehicle Crash Fatality Data." DVCIC - National Animal-Vehicle Crash Fatality Data. http://www.deercrash.org/states/national_data.htm

11. Minnesota Department of Natural Resources. "Frequently Asked Questions About Moose in Minnesota." http://files.dnr.state.mn.us/fish_wildlife/wildlife/moose/management/moosefaq.pdf

12. Strickland, Jessica. "Minnesota: Warmer Temperatures Take a Toll on Minnesota Moose." Open Spaces: A Blog of the Fish and Wildlife Service. http://www.fws.gov/news/blog/index.cfm/2011/5/17/Minnesota-Warmer-Temperatures-Take-a-Toll-on-Minnesota-Moose

13. Minnesota Department of Natural Resources. "Showy Lady's Slipper: Nature Snapshots from Minnesota DNR: Minnesota DNR." Showy Lady's Slipper: Nature Snapshots from Minnesota DNR: Minnesota DNR. http://www.dnr.state.mn.us/snapshots/plants/showyladysslipper.html

14. Minnesota Department of Natural Resources. "Plants That Eat Animals: March-April 2002." Young Naturalists: Plants That Eat Animals. http://www.dnr.state.mn.us/young_naturalists/insectivores/index.html

15. Crawford, Dave. "Brittle prickly pear (*Opuntia fragilis*)." Minnesota Profile. http://www.dnr.state.mn.us/volunteer/julaug09/mp.html

16. Marrone, Teresa, and Kathy Yerrich. *Mushrooms of the Upper Midwest: A Simple Guide to Common Mushrooms*. Cambridge, Minnesota: Adventure Publications, Inc., 2014.

Minnesota's 10,000 Lakes

1. Minnesota Department of Natural Resources. "Lakes, rivers, and wetlands facts." Lakes, rivers & wetlands: Minnesota Facts & Figures: Minnesota DNR. http://www.dnr.state.mn.us/faq/mnfacts/water.html

2. North Vancouver District Public Library. "Canadian Citizenship Test." http://www.nvdpl.ca/resource-guides/citizenship_test

3. Chrisfinke.com. "Does Minnesota really have more shoreline than California?" http://www.chrisfinke.com/2013/12/30/does-minnesota-really-have-more-shoreline-than-california/

4. Minnesota Department of Natural Resources. "Lakes, rivers, and wetlands facts." Lakes, rivers & wetlands: Minnesota Facts & Figures: Minnesota DNR. http://www.dnr.state.mn.us/faq/mnfacts/water.html

5. Gibbon, Guy E. *Archaeology of Minnesota: the Prehistory of the Upper Mississippi River Region*. Minneapolis: University of Minnesota Press, 2012.

6. Minnesota Department of Natural Resources. "Lakes, rivers, and wetlands facts." http://www.dnr.state.mn.us/faq/mnfacts/water.html

7. *Ibid.*

8. Rook.com. "BWCA Lakes." Index Page. http://www.rook.org/earl/bwca/lakes/#Format

9. Minnesota Department of Natural Resources. "Lakes, rivers, and wetlands facts." http://www.dnr.state.mn.us/faq/mnfacts/water.html

10. IDS-Center.com. "About IDS Center." http://www.ids-center.com/?page_id=11

11. Cook, Mark, and Jerry Younk. "A Recalculation of the Annual Statewide Recreational Fishing Effort and Harvest in Minnesota Lakes." http://files.dnr.state.mn.us/publications/fisheries/investigational_reports/493.pdf

12. *Ibid.*

13. Minnesota Department of Natural Resources. "Fish & fishing." http://www.dnr.state.mn.us/faq/mnfacts/fishing.html

14. Millelacs.com. "Minnesota Ice Fishing | Ice Fishing Houses | Lake Mille Lacs." http://millelacs.com/activities/icefish/

15. U.S. Census Bureau. "American FactFinder - Community Facts." American FactFinder - Community Facts. http://factfinder2.census.gov/faces/nav/jsf/pages/community_facts.xhtml

16. Zippelbay.com. "Zippel Bay Ice Fishing." http://www.zippelbay.com/icefishing2.htm

17. *Star Tribune*, "Beer Buzz? FAA Grounds Drone Plan," January 31, 2014.

18. Minnesota Department of Natural Resources. "Minnesota state record fish." http://www.dnr.state.mn.us/fishing/staterecords.html

19. *Ibid.*

20. Dave, Milles. "Pardon Me Myth! Who Owns the Lakebed?." http://files.dnr.state.mn.us/publications/waters/Pardon_Me_Myth.pdf

21. *Star Tribune*, "Alligator Surprises Anglers: Clyde the Alligator Was Killed by a DNR Officer in a Washington County Lake, but a Search Was Underway for Bonnie," August 30, 2013.

22. U.S. Geological Survey. "Red Piranha (*Pygocentrus nattereri*) - FactSheet." Red Piranha (*Pygocentrus nattereri*) - FactSheet. http://nas.er.usgs.gov/queries/FactSheet.aspx?SpeciesID=429

23. MyFoxTwinCities.com. "Alligator shot by Minnesota DNR near Scandia, hunt for one more." KMSP-TV. http://www.myfoxtwincities.com/story/23289852/goose-lake-gators-scandia-minnesota

24. Cione, Luis Alberto, et al. *Megapiranha paranensis*, a new genus and species of Serrasalmidae (Characiformes, Teleostei) from the upper Miocene of Argentina. *Journal of Vertebrate Paleontology*. Vol. 29, Iss. 2. 2009.

25. Rosaen, Alex, et al. "The Costs of Aquatic Invasive Species to Great Lakes States." http://www.nature.org/ourinitiatives/regions/northamerica/areas/greatlakes/ais-economic-report.pdf

26. Opefe.com. "State by State List of Statutes: Prohibit Piranha." State by State List of Statutes: Prohibit Piranha. http://www.opefe.com/state_stat_prohibit.html (accessed June 2, 2014)

27. Irons, Kevin. "Challenges of Nonnative Fishes in the Illinois River." http://ilrdss.isws.illinois.edu/pubs/govconf2011/session2c/Irons.pdf

28. Minnesota Pollution Control Agency. "Sources of mercury pollution and the methylmercury contamination of fish in Minnesota." http://www.pca.state.mn.us/

29. Minnesota Department of Health. "Fish Consumption: Frequently Asked Questions." http://www.health.state.mn.us/divs/eh/fish/faq.html#whatcontam

Lake Superior

1. Minnesota Sea Grant. "Lake Superior." Minnesota Sea Grant. http://www.seagrant.umn.edu/superior/

2. Duluth Seaway Port Authority | Port of Duluth-Superior. "The largest, farthest-inland freshwater port." http://www.duluthport.com/

3. Great Lakes St. Lawrence Seaway System. "Seaway Map." Seaway System. http://www.greatlakes-seaway.com/en/navigating/map/index.html

4. *Ibid.*

5. MacFarlane, Daniel. "Rapid Changes: Canada and the St. Lawrence Seaway and Power Project." http://powi.ca/wp-content/uploads/2012/12/Rapid-Changes-Canada-and-the-St.Lawrence-Sea-way-and-Power-Project.pdf

6. Hodgson, Bruce. "The Great Lakes St. Lawrence Seaway System." http://www.hwyh2o.com/pdf/ITMA Presentation Feb10_pdf.pdf

7. *Ibid.*

8. Great Canadian Rivers. "The St. Lawrence River." The St. Lawrence River. "Great Canadian Rivers." http://www.greatcanadianrivers.com/rivers/stlawer/economy-home.html

9. The St. Lawrence Seaway System Management Corporation. "The Seaway." http://www.seaway.ca/en/seaway/index.html

10. Environmental Protection Agency. "Water Trivia Facts." Home. http://water.epa.gov/learn/kids/drinking-water/water_trivia_facts.cfm

11. Minnesota Department of Natural Resources. "Lakes, rivers, and wetlands facts." http://www.dnr.state.mn.us/faq/mnfacts/water.html

12. Maritime-Connector. "Seawaymax." Jobs At Sea. http://maritime-connector.com/wiki/seawaymax/

13. Woods Hole Oceanographic Institution. "RMS Titanic." Woods Hole Oceanographic Institution. https://www.whoi.edu/main/topic/titanic

14. The St. Lawrence Seaway System Management Corporation. "A Vital Waterway." Seaway System. http://www.greatlakes-seaway.com/en/seaway/vital/index.html

15. Kates, Kristi. "Pirates of the Great Lakes." Pirates of the Great Lakes. http://www.northernexpress.com/michigan/article-6127-pirates-of-the-great-lakes.html

16. *The New York Times*, "Shot Stops a Lake "Pirate." June 30, 1908.

17. Boyd, Dr. Richard. "Roaring Dan Seavey." http://www.hsmichigan.org/wp-content/uploads/2012/04/DanSeavey.pdf

18. Gidmark, Jill B. *Encyclopedia of American literature of the sea and Great Lakes*. Westport, Conn.: Greenwood Press, 2001.

19. Great Lakes Distillery. "Great Lakes Distillery Recipes." http://www.greatlakesdistillery.com/cms/wp-content/uploads/downloads/2012/09/Signature-Cocktail-Recipes.pdf

20. Cameron, Jenks. *The Development of Governmental Forest Control in the United States*. Baltimore, MD: Johns Hopkins Press, 1928.

21. Rodgers, Bradley A. *Guardian of the Great Lakes: the U.S. paddle frigate Michigan*. Ann Arbor: University of Michigan Press, 1996.

22. NavSource. "NavSource Online: Gunboat Photo Archives." Gunboat Michigan DANFS page. http://www.navsource.org/archives/12/09905d.htm

23. *Ibid.*

24. National Oceanographic and Atmospheric Administration. "Annual Maximum Ice Cover." http://www.glerl.noaa.gov/data/ice/imgs/sup.jpg

25. *Ibid.*

26. NBC News. "Frozen-Over Lake Superior Provides Rare Access to Ice Caves—NBC News." http://www.nbcnews.com/storyline/deep-freeze/frozen-over-lake-superior-provides-rare-access-ice-caves-n31711

27. Third Coast Surf Shop. "Great Lakes Surfing FAQ." http://www.thirdcoastsurfshop.com/Great-Lakes-Surfing-FAQ-s/307.htm

28. National Oceanographic and Atmospheric Administration. "National Data Buoy Center." National Data Buoy Center. http://www.ndbc.noaa.gov

29. Continuous Wave. "Outrage 18 in Three-Foot Lake Huron Waves—Moderated Discussion Areas." http://continuouswave.com/ubb/Forum1/HTML/018843.html

30. Kent, Elizabeth. "Were extreme waves in the Rockall Trough the largest ever recorded?." *Geophysical Research Letters*.

31. Pinho, U. F. "Freak waves: more frequent than rare!" *Annales Geophysicae*: 1839-1842.

A Sampling of Lake Superior Shipwrecks

1. Boatnerd.com. "13. Lake Superior." Coast Pilot Chapter. http://www.boatnerd.com/facts-figures/lksuper.htm

2. Marshall, James R. *Shipwrecks of Lake Superior*. Duluth, Minn.: Lake Superior Port Cities, 2005.

3. Great Lakes Shipwreck Museum. "Shipwrecks." http://www.shipwreckmuseum.com/shipwrecks

4. Thompson, Mark L. *Graveyard of the Lakes*. Detroit: Wayne State University Press, 2000.

5. *Ibid.*

6. National Oceanographic and Atmospheric Administration. "NOAA Chart 14976." Chart 14976. http://www.charts.noaa.gov/OnLineViewer/14976.shtml

7. HathiTrust Digital Library. "Annual report of the Lake Carriers' Association, for the years 1908, 1911, 1913, 1914, and 1915." http://babel.hathitrust.org/cgi/pt?id=mdp.39015010732538;view=1up;seq=176;

8. Childs, Arcynta Ali. "A Michigan Museum of Shipwrecks." Smithsonian. http://www.smithsonianmag.com/travel/a-michigan-museum-of-shipwrecks-2152249/?no-ist

9. The Eastland Memorial Society. "Eastland Memorial Society." Eastland Memorial Society. http://www.eastlandmemorial.org/eastland2.shtml

10. Minnesota Sea Grant. "Lake Superior Holds Onto Her Dead ... and Her Toxaphene." http://www. seagrant.umn.edu/newsletter/2007/02/lake_superior_holds_onto_her_dead_and_her_toxaphene.html

11. Swayze, David D. "Great Lakes Shipwrecks beginning with the letter A." http://greatlakeshistory. homestead.com/files/a.htm

12. Marshall, James R. *Shipwrecks of Lake Superior.* Page 12. Duluth, MN: Lake Superior Port Cities, 2005.

13. *Ibid.*

14. *Ibid.*

15. *Ibid.*

16. Swayze, David D. "Great Lakes Shipwrecks beginning with the letter S." http://greatlakeshistory. homestead.com/files/a.htm

17. *Ibid.*

18. Wagenmaker, Richard, and Greg Mann. "The White Hurricane Storm of 1913: A Numerical Model Perspective." http://www.crh.noaa.gov/images/dtx/climate/1913Retrospective.pdf

19. National Weather Service, (Gaylord, MI). "Great Storms of the Great Lakes." http://www.crh.noaa.gov/ images/apx/presentations/Great_Storms_woNotes.pdf

20. *Ibid.*

21. U.S. Coast Guard/U.S. Department of Homeland Security. "U.S. Coast Guard Lightlist." http://www. navcen.uscg.gov/pdf/lightLists/LightList V7.pdf

22. Minnesota Department of Natural Resources. "State Parks." Minnesota Facts & Figures: Minnesota DNR. http://www.dnr.state.mn.us/faq/mnfacts/state_parks.html

23. Rowlett, Russ. "Lighthouses of the U.S.: Minnesota." Lighthouses of the U.S.: Minnesota. http://www. unc.edu/~rowlett/lighthouse/mn.htm. 2003.

24. Krueger, Andrew. "Lake Superior shipwreck find Scotiadoc is Great Lakes' deepest." *The Duluth News Tribune.*

25. Great Lakes Shipwreck Research. "Great Lakes Shipwreck Law." http://www.baillod.com/shipwreck/ projects/wrecklaw/

26. Swayze, David. "The Comet." http://www.ship-wreck.com/shipwreck/swayze/swayzedbdetail.php? HKEY=4101

27. Conley, Casey. "Largest laker runs aground bow-to-stern, blocking St. Marys River." *Professional Mariner.* http://www.professionalmariner.com/December-January-2013/Largest-laker-runs-aground-bow-to-stern-blocking-St-Marys-River/

28. Minnesota Department of Natural Resources. "Lake Superior Safety Information." http://www.dnr.state.mn.us/water_access/harbors/boatingsafety.html

29. National Transportation and Safety Board, Marine Accident Brief. "Sinking of the Tall Ship Bounty." https://www.ntsb.gov/doclib/reports/2014/MAB1403.pdf

30. Daniel, Stephen B. *Shipwrecks along Lake Superior's North Shore: a Diver's Guide.* St. Paul, MN: Minnesota Historical Society Press, 2008.

31. Minnesota Historical Society Press. "History of Inland Water Transportation in Minnesota; Minnesota's Inland Shipwrecks." http://www.mnhs.org/places/nationalregister/shipwrecks/mpdf/inship.html

32. *Ibid.*

33. Swayze, David. "S.S. Henry Steinbrenner." http://www.ship-wreck.com/shipwreck/swayze/swayzedbdetail.php?HKEY=249

34. *Ibid.*

35. Boatnerd.com. "The Sinking of the *Edmund Fitzgerald* November 10, 1975." http://www.boatnerd.com/fitz

36. Great Lakes Shipwreck Historical Society. "The Fateful Journey." http://www.shipwreckmuseum.com/the-fateful-journey-62/

37. *Ibid.*

38. SS *Edmund Fitzgerald* Online. "Memorials." http://www.ssefo.com/remembrances/memorials.html

39. National Weather Service Weather Forecast Office. "The Storm of November 9-11, 1998." http://www.crh.noaa.gov/mqt/?n=fitz_galesb

Minnesota Disasters

Asteroid Strikes

1. Minnesota Geological Survey. "Minnesota's Evidence of an Ancient Meteorite Impact." http://www.mngs.umn.edu/meteoriteimpact.pdf

2. United States Geological Survey. "Earthquake Calculator." earthquake.usgs.gov/learn/topics/calculator.php.

The Spanish Flu and Polio

1. Barry, JM. "The site of origin of the 1918 influenza pandemic and its public health implications. Barry JM. *Journal of Translational Medicine.* 2(1), January 20, 2004.

2. Minnesota State Board of Health. *Eighth Biennial Report (New Series) Of The State Board of Health And Vital Statistics Of Minnesota, 1918–1919.*

3. *Ibid.*

4. Navarro, JA. "Influenza in 1918: An Epidemic in Images." *Public Health Reports*. April 2010. http://www.ncbi.nlm.nih.gov/pubmed/20568565/

5. The Great War, Public Broadcasting System. "WW I Casualties and Death Tables." http://www.pbs.org/greatwar/resources/casdeath_pop.html

6. Minnesota Department of Health. "Polio: Minnesota's Critical Role." http://www.health.state.mn.us/library/dhsjournals/Chapter3.pdf

7. *Ibid.*

8. *Ibid.*

9. Global Polio Eradication Initiative. "Oral Polio Vaccine Supply." http://www.polioeradication.org/Financing/Budgetcomponents/Oralpoliovaccinesupply.aspx

Smallpox and Other Diseases

1. Hodge, Adam R. 2010. "Pestilence and Power: The Smallpox Epidemic of 1780–1782 and Intertribal Relations on the Northern Great Plains." *Historian* 72, no. 3: 543-567.

2. *Ibid.*

3. Riedel, Stefan. "Edward Jenner and the History of Smallpox and Vaccination." *Proceedings of Baylor University Medical Center.* 18: 21-25.

4. Mann, Charles. "1491." *The Atlantic*. Atlantic Media Company, 1 Mar. 2002. http://www.theatlantic.com/magazine/archive/2002/03/1491/302445/

5. *George Washington's Mount Vernon.* "Smallpox." http://www.mountvernon.org/educational-resources/encyclopedia/smallpox

6. Mann, Charles. "1491." *The Atlantic*. Atlantic Media Company, 1 Mar. 2002. Web. 2 June 2014. http://www.theatlantic.com/magazine/archive/2002/03/1491/302445/

7. Nelson, Paul. "Smallpox epidemic of 1924-25 claimed the lives of 500 Minnesotans." MinnPost. http://www.minnpost.com/mnopedia/2014/03/smallpox-epidemic-1924-25-claimed-lives-500-minnesotans

8. Minnesota State Department of Health. "Conquered and Almost-Conquered Diseases." http://www.health.state.mn.us/library/dhsjournals/Chapter2.pdf

9. Minnesota Encyclopedia, Minnesota Historical Society. "Establishment of the Minneapolis Waterworks, 1867–1910." Accessed June 2, 2014. http://www.mnopedia.org/thing/establishment-minneapolis-water-works-1867-1910

10. Goodell, John. "Minnesota's Typhoid Fever Record." *American Water Works Association* 7: 280-282. http://www.jstor.org/stable/41224654?seq=3

11. Armstrong, John. "The Asiatic Cholera in St. Paul." *Minnesota History*. September, 1933.

12. *Ibid.*

13. Wesbrook, F. F. "Diphtheria Infection In Minnesota. Recent Experiences With The Disease In School Children And In Institutional Epidemics." *JAMA: The Journal of the American Medical Association*: 939-943

Mine Disasters and Other Catastrophes

1. NewsHopper. "Milford Mine Disaster." http://crowwing.us/DocumentCenter/Home/View/118

2. *Ibid.*

3. Centers for Disease Control and Prevention. "Metal/Nonmetal Mining Disasters: 1869 to Present." Centers for Disease Control and Prevention. http://www.cdc.gov/niosh/mining/statistics/content/mnmdisasters.html

4. Trennery, Walter. "The Minnesota Legislature and the Grasshopper: 1873-1877." http://collections.mnhs.org/MNHistoryMagazine/articles/36/v36i02p054-061.pdf.

5. *Ibid.*

Plane Crashes

1. National Transportation Safety Board. "Controlled Collision with Terrain: Northwest Airlink Flight 5719 http://www.airdisaster.com/reports/ntsb/AAR94-05.pdf

2. Travel + Leisure. "America's Safest Airports." http://www.travelandleisure.com/articles/americas-safest-airports

I-35W Bridge Disaster

1. National Transportation Safety Board. "Collapse of I-35W Bridge, National Transportation Safety Board Accident Report." http://www.dot.state.mn.us/i35wbridge/ntsb/finalreport.pdf

2. FEMA. "U.S. Fire Administration Technical Report Series, I-35W Bridge Collapse and Response." https://www.usfa.fema.gov/downloads/pdf/publications/tr_166.pdf

Fires

1. National Oceanographic and Atmospheric Administration. "Glossary Entry for Temperature Inversion." http://w1.weather.gov/glossary/index.php?word=temperature+inversion

2. The City of Hinckley. "The Great Hinckley Fire of 1894." http://www.hinckley.govoffice2.com/index.asp?-Type=B_BASIC&SEC=%7BFD8DC19D-5036-4403-8C87-061FFE2E781A%7D

3. Wilkinson, William. *Memorials of the Minnesota forest fires in the year 1894: with a chapter on the forest fires in Wisconsin in the same year.* Minneapolis: N.E. Wilkinson, 1895.

4. The City of Hinckley. "The Great Hinckley Fire of 1894." http://www.hinckley.govoffice2.com/index.asp?-Type=B_BASIC&SEC=%7BFD8DC19D-5036-4403-8C87-061FFE2E781A%7D

5. *Ibid*.

6. Minnesota Historical Society. "The Great Fires of 1918, MN 150." http://discovery.mnhs.org/MN150/index.php?title=The_Great_Fires_of_1918

7. Rogers, David. "How Geologists Unraveled the Mystery of Japanese Vengeance Balloon Bombs in World War II." http://web.mst.edu/~rogersda/forensic_geology/japenese vengenance bombs new.htm

8. Rizzo, Johnna. "Japan's Secret WWII Weapon: Balloon Bombs." National Geographic. http://news.nationalgeographic.com/news/2013/05/130527-map-video-balloon-bomb-wwii-japanese-air-current-jet-stream/

Mill and Industrial Disasters

1. Mill City Museum. "Building History." Mill City Museum. http://www.millcitymuseum.org/building-history

2. Pennefeather, Shannon. *Mill City: A Visual History Of The Minneapolis Mill District*. Minnesota Historical Society Press. 2003.

3. Winkley's Orthotics and Prosthetics. "Family History." History. http://www.winkley.com/our-history/

Other Disasters and Accidents of Note

1. *Reading Eagle*. "Santa Claus Unhurt as Plane Crashes." December 18, 1949.

Crime

1. Meier, Peg. "The Shame of Minneapolis." *Star Tribune*, January 8, 2003.

2. *Ibid*.

3. Chestnutt Archive. "Lynchings by State." http://www.chesnuttarchive.org/classroom/lynchings_table_state.html

4. *The Appeal*. "3,000 Lynchings in Twenty Years." September 14, 1901. http://chroniclingamerica.loc.gov/lccn/sn83016810/1901-09-14/ed-1/seq-1/

5. Minnesota Historical Society. "Duluth Lynchings Online Resource: Timeline." Duluth Lynchings Online Resource: Timeline. http://collections.mnhs.org/duluthlynchings/html/text_timeline.htm

6. *Ibid*.

7. Burgan, Michael. *Famous Crimes of Minnesota*. Cambridge, MN: Adventure Publications, 2013.

8. South Dakota Public Broadcasting. "Paul Maccabee Interview." http://www.sdpb.sd.gov/vernemiller/maccabee.asp

9. Burgan, Michael. *Famous Crimes of Minnesota.* Cambridge, MN: Adventure Publications, 2013.

10. *Ibid.*

11. Federal Bureau of Investigation. "Latent Prints in the 1933 Hamm Kidnapping." http://www.fbi.gov/news/stories/2003/september/hamm090803

12. Federal Bureau of Investigation. "The Lindbergh Kidnapping." FBI. http://www.fbi.gov/about-us/history/famous-cases/the-lindbergh-kidnapping

13. *Ibid.*

A Brief Look at Sports

1. "Minnesota Twins Team History and Encyclopedia." Baseballreference.com. http://www.baseball-reference.com/teams/MIN/

2. Ibid.

3. Nathan, Alan M. "Revisiting Mantle's Griffith Stadium Home Run." http://baseball.physics.illinois.edu/Krannert-v3.pdf

4. Minnesota Twins. "Minnesota Twins Tickets." http://minnesota.twins.mlb.com/ticketing

5. "Minnesota Vikings Franchise Encyclopedia." Pro-football-reference.com. http://www.pro-football-reference.com/teams/min/

6. "NFL Career Points Scored Leaders." Pro-football-reference.com. http://www.pro-football-reference.com/leaders/scoring_career.htm

7. "Alan Page NFL Football Statistics." Pro-football-reference.com. http://www.pro-football-reference.com/players/P/PageAl00.htm

8. "Minnesota Timberwolves Franchise Index. Basketball-reference.com " http://www.basketball-reference.com/teams/MIN/

9. "Wolves' Kevin Love talks about his uncle's Beach Boys." Twincities.com. http://www.twincities.com/sports/ci_19595495

10. "Minnesota Wild Franchise Encyclopedia." Hockey-reference.com. http://www.hockey-reference.com/teams/MIN/

11. "What If? Wild Uniforms." Minnesotawild.com. http://wild.nhl.com/club/gallerylanding.htm?id=20535

Quirky Minnesota

1. Office of the Revisor of Statutes. "2013 Minnesota Statutes, 97C.601. https://www.revisor.mn.gov/statutes/?id=97C.601&year=2013

2. Office of the Revisor of Statutes. "145.365 Trafficking in Skunks." https://www.revisor.mn.gov/statutes/?id=145.365&year=2013

3. Office of the Revisor of Statutes. "149A.72 Funeral Industry Practices; Misrepresentations." https://www.revisor.mn.gov/statutes/?id=149A.72&year=2013

4. Office of the Revisor of Statutes. "169.22 Hitchhiking; Solicitation of Business. " https://www.revisor.mn.gov/statutes/?id=169.22&year=2013&keyword_type=all&keyword=hitchhiking

5. Office of the Revisor of Statutes. "609.36 Adultery." https://www.revisor.mn.gov/statutes/?id=609.36&year=2013&keyword_type=all&keyword=adultery

6. Office of the Revisor of Statutes. "609.34 Fornication." https://www.revisor.mn.gov/statutes/?id=609.34&year=2013

7. Office of the Revisor of Statutes. "181.75 Polygraph Tests of Employees or Prospective Employees Prohibited." https://www.revisor.mn.gov/statutes/?id=181.75&year=2013

8. Office of the Revisor of Statutes. "617.23 Indecent Exposure; Penalties." https://www.revisor.mn.gov/statutes/?id=617.23&year=2013

9. Office of the Revisor of Statutes. "550.37 Property Exempt." https://www.revisor.mn.gov/statutes/?id=550.37&year=2013

10. Office of the Revisor of Statutes. "145.425 Pay Toilets in Public Places." https://www.revisor.mn.gov/statutes/?id=145.425&year=2013

11. Office of the Revisor of Statutes. "97C.605 Turtles." https://www.revisor.mn.gov/statutes/?id=97C.605&year=2013

12. Office of the Revisor of Statutes. "609.71 Riot." https://www.revisor.mn.gov/statutes/?id=609.71&year=2013

13. Office of the Revisor of Statutes. "97B.645 Wolves." https://www.revisor.mn.gov/statutes/?id=97B.645&year=2013&keyword_type=all&keyword=donkey

14. "St. Urho, Legendary Patron Saint of Finland." http://www.sainturho.com/mattson.htm

15. Guinness World Records. "Largest gathering of zombies." http://www.guinnessworldrecords.com/records-5000/largest-gathering-of-zombies/

16. Minnesota State Legislature. "Looking back: 'Fast time' causes tense time at Capitol." http://www.house.leg.state.mn.us/hinfo/swkly/1995-96/select/time.txt

17. Minnesota State Legislature. "103G.651 Removing Sunken Logs from Public Waters." https://www.revisor.mn.gov/statutes/?id=103G.651&year=2013

18. Lowry, Ray. "Hill's Folly; The Building of the Stone Arch Bridge." http://www.gngoat.org/stone_arch_bridge.htm

19. CBS Interactive. "The Odd Truth: Feb. 13, 2004." http://www.cbsnews.com/news/the-odd-truth-feb-13-2004/

20. Roadside America. "Eveleth, MN: World's Largest Free-Standing Hockey Stick." RoadsideAmerica.com. http://www.roadsideamerica.com/tip/717

21. Roadside America. "Big Smokey Bear, International Falls, Minnesota." RoadsideAmerica.com. http://www.roadsideamerica.com/story/2132

22. Roadside America. "North St. Paul, Minnesota: World's Largest Stucco Snowman." http://www.road-sideamerica.com/tip/724

23. Roadside America. "Minnesota Tourist Attractions." http://www.roadsideamerica.com/location/mn

About the Author

Brett Ortler is the author of *The Fireflies Book* and *The Mosquito Book*. An editor at Adventure Publications, he has edited dozens of books, including many field guides and nature-themed books. His work appears widely, including in *Salon*, *The Good Men Project*, *The Nervous Breakdown*, *Living Ready* and in a number of other venues in print and online. He lives in the Twin Cities with his wife and their young son. For more, visit www.brettortler.com.